We all experience challenging seasons in our lives when we can allow them to either debilitate us or spur us on to growth. Diana Pintimalli, in her book *In Between*, eloquently weaves godly wisdom, counsel, and practical tips on the tapestry of her vulnerable healing journey during a difficult season of her life. This is an encouraging, honest, uplifting must-read for every person who finds themself in an in-between place and would like to harvest good fruit from it.

—Rita Della Civita, MA
Psychotherapist, Isaiah 40 Foundation

We often confuse destination with journey. In life, we look to hitting certain destinations as a marker of success when what we really mean is how well we are doing on life's journey. Consider Diana's book as a go-to resource for your life's journey. Her guidance will provide you with all the things you need to make the most of the trip.

—Jonathan DiStaulo, MA, LPC
Foundations Counseling & Consulting, LLC

IN

Between

IN

Between

FINDING PEACE
AND STRENGTH IN THE MIDST
OF LIFE'S CONTINUOUS MOTIONS

DIANA PINTIMALLI

IN BETWEEN
Copyright © 2022 by Diana Pintimalli

Unless otherwise indicated, all Scripture quotations have been taken from the Christian Standard Bible®, Copyright © 2017 by Holman Bible Publishers. Used by permission. Christian Standard Bible® and CSB® are federally registered trademarks of Holman Bible Publishers. Scripture quotations marked KJV taken from the Holy Bible, King James Version, which is in the public domain. Scripture taken from the New King James Version®. Copyright © 1982 by Thomas Nelson. Used by permission. All rights reserved. Scripture quotations marked (NIV) are taken from the Holy Bible, New International Version®, NIV®. Copyright © 1973, 1978, 1984, 2011 by Biblica, Inc.® Used by permission of Zondervan. All rights reserved worldwide. www.zondervan.com The "NIV" and "New International Version" are trademarks registered in the United States Patent and Trademark Office by Biblica, Inc.®

ISBN: 978-1-4866-2155-2
eBook ISBN: 978-1-4866-2156-9

Word Alive Press
119 De Baets Street Winnipeg, MB R2J 3R9
www.wordalivepress.ca

WORD ALIVE
—P R E S S—

Cataloguing in Publication information can be obtained from Library and Archives Canada.

This book is dedicated to my husband Benny, and my children Sarah and Brandon, who have stood beside me every step of this journey. I am forever grateful for your unconditional love and support.

I want to thank T.L.C. for all your prayers throughout the years. I love you.

CONTENTS

PREFACE

HAVE YOU EVER FELT STUCK? TIRED, OVERWHELMED, PHYSICALLY and mentally burned out? Finding yourself in a difficult situation, feeling like you can't get away from it?

I know that I'm not the only one who at one time or another has been stuck in the *in between*. Throughout my journey, I've had the opportunity to speak with many people who have one thing in common: being stuck. They were either stuck in a situation, a career or marriage they were unhappy with, or stuck in a mindset that didn't allow them to live and be truly alive. They were set in a particular way of thinking and unable to change their mind, because they didn't want to deal with something unpleasant.

Rather than deal with the problem, people often settle and choose to stay in an uncomfortable situation. However, in some weird way they *are* comfortable. They would rather not explore any other option, even if it could bring healing.

Being *in between* means to be in a middle position, to be situated somewhere between two extremes. In some cases, it means being in between success and failure.

A good example of this are tweens. Tweens are often at an *in between* stage, neither a child nor an adult. They're in the midst of becoming. It's an *in between* stage of life.

My *in between* stage happened in my late thirties. I was in an almost constant state of physical and mental exhaustion, which eventually turned into burnout and feelings of anxiety. I later learned that this was caused by excessive and prolonged stress. I was overwhelmed and unable to meet the constant daily demands placed upon me. I felt emotionally drained and exhausted. I knew I was on the verge of burnout because of my lack of energy. I felt tired and forgetful most days. I had insomnia, trouble concentrating, and unexplained sadness and anxiety.

The sadness paralyzed me. I asked myself, *How can I be sad? How can I feel this way? I have God in my life. I have a great life, a husband, children, friends, a career… and all my loved ones are safe and healthy. I'm not suffering from any life-threatening illness. I'm alive and breathing.*

So why did I feel this way? I didn't know the answer in that moment, but throughout my *in between* journey, I got it. Let me take you on my journey and explore how I was freed from burnout through faith, belief, rest, and perseverance. As I tell my story, you'll be able to see how I got through it and even enjoyed my *in between* process.

INTRODUCTION

IT WAS A VERY COMMON THURSDAY MORNING ON A CRISP JANUARY day. I woke up as usual at the sound of my alarm going off at 6:00 a.m. Still tired from not having had a very restful night's sleep, tormented from dreaming of all the endless demands at work and home that needed to be met, and waking up to the reality of these demands left me with the same lump in my throat I always had when I felt anxiety coming on, a throbbing headache still lingering from the night before, and the physical pain of aching bones as I dragged myself out of bed.

This day was slightly different in routine, though, since I had my annual appointment with my doctor. This day would demand more of me. Time was tight and the children needed to be ready more quickly in order for me to still make it to work on time. I had unrealistically scheduled the doctor's appointment very early in the morning just so I wouldn't have to miss work and end up having to depend on someone else to help out.

As challenging as the morning was, I made it to my doctor's appointment. Stressed but nonetheless on time.

As I sat on the dingy wooden chair in the semi-crowded and stale-smelling waiting room, I stared out at the other patients. My eyes fixed on the tape at the corner of the used-up carpet so no one would see the tears starting to form in my eyes. Guilt crept up as I thought about my children and how I had treated them earlier. Sadness overwhelmed me when I remembered how I had treated my husband who had only been trying to help out and make things easier. My own words echoed in my mind as I prayed for forgiveness.

When my name was called, I gathered my belongings and pulled myself together to enter the doctor's office. I reminded myself that I didn't want to show him any defeat.

All he asked was "How are you today?"

I could hardly get the words out of my mouth. I knew that if I told him the truth about how I felt, physically and mentally, my life would drastically change.

Thinking of the destruction and devastation my actions would cause my family made me shake and recoil. I tried so hard to hold back emotional words and not tell him the truth. In that moment, I knew I couldn't handle any additional change or demand; I couldn't take the ones I already had. For months, my work life had been exhausting, demanding, and completely boundaryless. I couldn't take another day of meeting unrealistic expectations.

I was scared to speak up because my home life was good, even somewhat easy. Or was it? Who was it easy for? For myself? My family? My husband and children?

That's when it happened. I opened my mouth and couldn't control my words or emotions. Tears rolled down my cheeks, as though I was mourning a loved one.

"I'm fine, Doctor," I said. "All good with me. Just rushed and stressed, but nothing I can't handle."

I tried to hide it, tried to control my emotions, to make it seem like I was just having a bad morning.

But the truth took over. I started to spill every detail of my life, details of months of heaviness and burdens, tears, and sadness.

I didn't like what I was feeling. I was full of confusion, despair, and guilt. Every time I tried to explain that I would be okay, that I just needed a few minutes to get myself together, even more tears rolled down and more words came out of my mouth.

He listened, let me finish, then gave me a concerned look. After further questions and discussion, he said, "I'm writing you up a leave of absence from work, effective immediately."

He went on to explain that I needed the time to recharge and make myself find pleasure in life again. He recommended that I start with a break and re-evaluate the situation monthly.

It was crazy how scared I felt. It felt as though he was telling me I had some life-threatening disorder.

"From time to time, people need some time to take a step back and recharge," he said.

In my case, he thought I need a longer than usual amount of time.

I left his office not knowing where to start. I knew that the decision to take a break would upset many people in my life. I would be letting them down.

I had never done anything like this before. I was always the strong one, the compliant one, the one to whom people turned to get things done. I felt nervous, because I didn't know how to set limits in my life. I had never expressed any form of boundaries with my employer and I most certainly had never expressed how exhausted I was.

And that day I was about to do both.

But the doctor had insisted that I take time off work.

I began to feel a sense of relief, like a responsibility had been lifted off my shoulders. I felt as though someone else was making the decision and choosing this for me. By shifting the responsibility for this decision from myself to my doctor, I hoped others would be better able to accept the decision. After all, I wasn't the one making it.

The drive into work that morning included many tears and phone calls to my husband and to my best friend, the only other person apart from my husband who knew me inside out, especially when it came to work. Not only did we have a beautiful friendship outside the office, we also celebrated the fact that we had worked together for many years. My days at the office were most definitely worth it because of her. I cherished her friendship, listening ear, and advice. She was—and is—one of the very special gifts I have received from God.

Neither my husband nor best friend were confused about what I was about to do, but they were very surprised. It wasn't like me to make a decision like this, let alone one so life-changing. But nothing could change my mind. I desperately needed this break, or else I'd end up broken.

And so I chose to do the unthinkable. I told my employer I would be taking a break. I explained everything that had been happening to lead me to this decision.

I stepped out of the office that day and never looked back.

Over the next few weeks and months, my guilt and shame produced a lot of anxiety. I felt as though the break was worse than the burnout had been. I felt guilty for being at home trying to improve myself, trying to regain my strength. I blamed myself for where I was in life, for what was happening to me. I blamed myself for doing this to my family, to my husband and children. I felt guilty for leaving work, for leaving my employer so abruptly, for leaving my co-workers who over the years had become like a second family.

I no longer feel that way now that I've been freed from guilt during my *in between* journey.

Throughout my journey, I've taken the time to research and study many books, including the Bible. Along the way I came across the book of James and realized that this book has abundant teachings from God about pursuing the life He wants us to enjoy.

James 1:5 tells us, *"Now if any of you lacks wisdom, he should ask God—who gives to all generously and ungrudgingly—and it will be given to him."* That's exactly what I did. I asked God for help, and out of my sincere and faithful request I have received these beautiful words. I give all the credit to God, who is my creator, my teacher, my comforter, my guide, and my peace.

I pray that each reader out there who may be going through their own *in between* will peacefully enjoy the journey as they move into the next stage of their life. If you've ever asked yourself one of these questions—what is my purpose? why am I here? is this what my life is all about?—then I encourage you to continue into the next few chapters and read with an open mind. I ask for an open mind because I often reference scriptures from the Bible. I believe it to be the truth and I find comfort in what is written there.

My words are meant for everyone, regardless of your beliefs and opinions. I pray you can embrace each word with love so that together we can guide those who are stuck. I truly believe that we are meant to help each other, whether it's through listening, encouraging, or guiding others.

My *in between* journey called for time off to recover and regain my physical and mental strength, but this won't be necessary for everyone. I encourage you to explore, investigate, and dig deep within yourself to find the peace that does exist but has been lost somewhere *in between*.

One
GRACE

LET ME INTRODUCE YOU TO GRACE. GRACE ISN'T A SPECIFIC PERSON with a specific name and specific face. However, she's a woman, mother, wife, sister, daughter, and friend. She is one of us. She's living—or should I say, surviving—a quite ordinary life. She eats, sleeps, prays, loves, laughs, cries, worries, hopes, dreams, cares, and works… the list could go on.

Like many of us, Grace goes about her regular routine. Then one day it happens: she notices that she's stuck. Stuck in the *in between*. How did this happen? Well, for starters, Grace is stuck because the idea of actually moving forward means change, and change, as we all know, can be scary. It sometimes feel safer to keep standing still.

Why can't we stay in a safe, stuck place? Well, if we did that, we would never get to experience the true beauty of what God has to offer us in our lives.

From my own experience, having a child has been one of the scariest forms of moving forward. The truth is that if I hadn't allowed myself to take that step, I would have missed out on two of the most precious gifts God has ever given me.

But no matter how long we study this stuck feeling, we can all admit that from time to time it does happen. Sometimes it lasts longer than others, and other times it lasts mere seconds.

One thing I can tell you is that we don't have to remain stuck.

Please allow me to tell you how Grace discovered freedom—but it didn't happen overnight.

Over the years, Grace unknowingly developed a passive aggressive attitude towards her job. She didn't do anything about it at first and instead remained in her unsatisfying career and unbalanced lifestyle. She was not living her purpose, and suddenly she realized she had gotten stuck and was unable to move. She couldn't even breathe properly at times.

Grace was left confused and saddened by these feelings because she couldn't understand what was happening. She had always been strong-willed, capable of making big decisions. People had even gone to Grace seeking advice. So how could it be that she started feeling like this?

Grace questioned herself and wondered about what she should do. Well, there are a number of solutions, but most importantly she first had to acknowledge that she had to walk through the *in between* process. She realized that she would never get to any destination by just staying in one place.

With that, she set off on her journey, fearful and nervous—yet hopeful and faithful.

Grace knew from experience that before setting off on a trip she had to prepare for it, getting clear directions in order to navigate her way to her destination. In her *in between* journey, she would have to plan, research, study, read, and pray.

Like Grace, we all have daily demands that need to be met, and sometimes we just don't know how to function. We try to balance work, pleasure, and everyday life at the same time. This can create stress.

Stress isn't always bad. In small and healthy doses, stress can help us perform daily tasks and motivate us to perform at our best.

But the word itself can trigger us. It's important to recognize unhealthy stress indicators in our lives, since unhealthy stress can lead to sickness and illness. Our bodies are designed to protect us, and so we all have a stress response that helps us stay focused, alert, and energetic in stressful situations, giving us the extra strength we need in order to pull through.

However, beyond a certain point stress can be damaging to our mood, relationships, health, and overall quality of life.

When our bodies are in fight-or-flight mode, it can affect our nervous systems, which causes our hearts to beat faster, our muscles to tighten, our blood pressure to rise, and our breath to quicken and grow short.

In Grace's case, her chest muscles would tighten and make breathing difficult. This would send her to the doctor, trying to figure out how seriously to take her chest pains.

These indicators leave us with a decision to make: either leave a stressful situation or stay in it. For Grace, her nervous system wasn't very good at identifying the difference between work stress and true life-or-death situations; the more her emergency stress system was activated, the harder it was to shut it off and choose to leave.

Grace tended to get stressed out a lot. In fact, her body existed in a state of stress most of the time. This eventually led to burnout. Her chronic stress levels left her feeling highly vulnerable to anxiety, depression, and other health issues. She developed sleep problems, chronic muscle aches and pains over her whole body, digestive problems, and memory problems. She had an inability to concentrate, constant worrying, racing thoughts, and many sleepless nights.

The ironic thing about Grace is that until she recognized her *in between* status, she had believed she only knew how to function when she was in a stressed state. Once she accepted her reality, she had to find another way to live. She had to learn to enjoy and just be.

Grace learned along the way that in order to move out of being stuck, she had to go to the place where it had all started. And for Grace, that was her childhood. She wasn't aware of the tools that were available to her—simple tools, available at no cost.

SIX ESSENTIAL TOOLS

Here are some of the tools Grace used to help deal with and manage stress.

> **1. Supportive network.** A very important tool is having a supportive network, such as family members and friends. In stressful situations, they can be an enormous benefit. When we have people we can lean on, life's pressures don't seem as overwhelming. With a reliable support network, we don't have to feel alone and frightened. They can help us shift our perspective, allowing us to dissect stressful situations and make light of them.

> **2. Perspective.** Our perspective and outlook on life can make a difference in our ability to handle stress, which is what makes having a healthy perspective another great tool to help us overcome stress. What you believe to be true about a situation is going to affect you.

3. Confidence. Confidence is another important tool. If we have confidence in ourselves, we are better able to conquer and persevere through challenges. Having the confidence to admit what is going on in our lives is the beginning of healing.

As a child, Grace did not know how to bring her emotions to light and speak about how she felt. Every time she felt an emotion, she hid it. She would either ignore it or try dealing with it on her own.

4. Physical activity. Moving around and exercising is another important tool to relieve stress. Regular exercise can lift up our moods and distract us from our worries, giving our minds a break from the stress. Daily walks can help relieve stress as well. Taking a small walk during the day can prevent a person from having increased anxiety.

5. Healthy diet. A healthy diet is another important tool that can improve our ability to cope through life's stresses. However, an unhealthy diet can worsen our mood and affect our ability to cope.

6. Rest. Rest can help us feel less stressed, more productive, and emotionally balanced. God encourages us to rest in His peace. In Matthew 11:28, Jesus tells us, *"Come to me, all of you who are weary and burdened, and I will give you rest."* He's saying that we just need to give all our burdens and anxieties to God, and He will give us the rest we need to go on.

Yet some people don't do that, thinking it's crazy and unrealistic to give our problems over to God. So instead people take matters into their own hands and try to control their stress, making it either worse or not helping it at all.

When Grace chose not to release her worries and burdens to God, her sleep became very ineffective, creating more anxiety.

Let us now explore each tool more deeply and apply them to our daily lives so, like Grace, we can live the life God intended for us to have in the first place.

SUPPORTIVE NETWORK

Admitting to our loved ones that we're stressed and burnt out is an important step in the journey. Sometimes people feel ashamed to tell others the truth about what's happening in their lives. Both fear and pride creep in front of us, preventing us from being honest and accepting the support we would most likely get from these people if we were honest with them.

Family makes for a wonderful support system. Talking to a loved one about a situation can help tremendously. Sharing and bringing feelings to light and voicing what's really going on allows something inside us to change. Our emotions shift, allowing us to get a different perspective on the situation.

PERSPECTIVE

Which brings me to the second tool, which is perspective. When I use this word, I'm talking about our point of view.

In reality, our point of view gives us the ability to either move toward a goal or move away from it. We're at an advantage with this tool, because we control it. We get to determine how we view a situation.

That said, this tool should be used in a positive manner. In many stressful situations, we choose to complain and nag. But we can instead choose to be positive and find the good in the situation. Nagging can become a habit, and before we know it we're trapped by a nagging perspective.

The Bible has plenty to say about nagging. Proverbs 25:24 says, *"Better to live on the corner of a roof than to share a house* with a nagging wife," and Proverbs 27:15 adds, "An endless dripping on a rainy day and a nagging wife are alike."

In the second verse, the author compares a gloomy rainy day to a nagging wife. We all know how long and dreadful a rainy day can be! It can alter all of our emotions. Just stop and think about it. Close your eyes and imagine the cold, constant dripping of the rain. How dreadful and sad.

The Bible also gives us the solution to negative and nagging people. We are to watch the words we say and speak only words that edify. Ephesians 4:29 says, "No foul language should come from your mouth, but only what is good for building up someone in need..." We're specifically told to use our words to build up. If we could truly learn to put that into practice, we would see victory at the end of every day.

CONFIDENCE

The third tool we will explore is confidence. Confidence comes from the Latin word *fidere*, which means to trust. Having self-confidence and trusting ourselves is very important. We must believe in ourselves, even when no one else believes in us, and stand firm in our belief, not allowing our perspective to shift even when others don't share those same beliefs.

Having just the right amount of confidence is tricky, though. Going around with an overconfident attitude can come across as arrogance. On the other hand, having too little confidence can stop you from pursuing your dream, seizing a career opportunity, or enjoying an amazing social life.

Practicing the proper amount of confidence, and making sure to take the time to project just enough confidence to deal with all challenges, whether they be personal or professional, is very important.

How can one practice confidence? Here are a few ways.

Smile at others and look them in the eyes, especially when speaking to them. Smiling shows others that you have a certain confidence, warmth, and ease about you. Also, you can use your smile during telephone conversations; you'd be surprised how easily one can tell if the other caller is smiling on their end of the line.

PHYSICAL ACTIVITY

To exercise is to carry out an activity requiring physical effort to improve one's health and fitness.

There are many benefits to physical exercise, such as helping us feel happier. It can also help with weight loss. It's good for our muscles and bones, too, and increases our energy level. It can reduce one's risk of chronic disease, promote healthy skin, help with brain health and memory, and lead to a better quality of sleep.

HEALTHY DIET

In order to maintain our happiness and reduce anxiety and depression, it's important to maintain a healthy diet. This means eating a healthy variety of foods that provide us with the nutrients we need to have good health and feel good. Healthy food gives us energy.

It's easy to get discouraged and off-track from maintaining a healthy lifestyle. However, if we choose the proper mindset and try a little harder, we can stay on track and follow a healthy daily routine.

With all the many diets and food choices we have available to us, it can sometimes be hard to know what diet to follow. But everyone is designed differently, requiring specific nutrients.

If necessary, meet with a well-respected, certified, and knowledgeable nutritionist. Have a discussion with them regarding healthy nutrition for your lifestyle. I don't believe any single way of eating is better than another, but I do believe in the importance of maintaining healthy nutrition to feed our bodies.

REST

To rest means to cease from work and cease from movement, in order to relax our bodies and refresh ourselves. Rest helps us to recover our strength.

There are quite a few benefits from getting proper rest, including better concentration, greater productivity, greater athletic performance, more energy, better mental function, lower risk of heart disease, and the ability to prevent depression. These are just a few of the many benefits.

Once Grace started to implement these tools, her life shifted and changed. Her sleep became restful, food became flavourful again, and life felt more peaceful. Her perspective shifted and Grace acted differently. She smiled at others, even giving compliments to strangers throughout the day. She took the time to thank and compliment the checkout person at a store she visited. She also started to notice what others around her did and gave them compliments as well.

Grace started practicing appreciation. She took the time to notice strangers who held the door open, and some who even gave her the chance to pass them at the checkout line. Once Grace chose to take her eyes off herself and give unselfishly of herself to others, more aspects of her life began to shift.

The Bible teaches that grace is a gift from God—as indicated in Ephesians 2:8, which says, *"For you are saved by grace through faith, and this is not from yourselves; it is God's gift"*—Grace came to realize that her healing was beginning. This time, she set effective and realistic goals—and achieved them.

Previously Grace tended to set herself up for disappointment. She agreed to commitments she already knew she wouldn't be able to follow through on, and she agreed to goals that would end up being destructive to her.

Two
PRAYER

PRAYER IS ONE OF THE MOST IMPORTANT TOOLS IN MY LIFE. THERE are many prayers I offer to God—prayers of thankfulness, healing, forgiveness, guidance, strength, hope, and protection.

I used to think that in order to pray, I should get down on my knees and shut the door of my room. But this made it quite difficult for me to even want to pray.

I then realized that praying comes in many different forms.

I like to think of prayer as a confidential conversation between myself and God, and there are no limits to what I can say. The truth is that God already hears all our thoughts, but taking the time to actually set apart time from our busy schedules is something special between us and God.

When praying, it helps when I set a quiet environment for myself. I select a specific place daily, too, and this makes my prayer time special, uplifting, and enjoyable.

I view prayer pretty much the same way I view having a conversation with a friend. The best ones take place when I'm free from distractions and completely connecting with the other person. The same is true during my prayer time. Freeing myself from distractions and preparing for my conversation with God allows me to not only speak but listen and be still as I wait on Him.

Here are some ways I prepare for a prayer conversation.

Sometimes I play soft instrumental worship music as I look through my Bible with a pen and paper close by. I like to write down the thoughts that come to me during my prayer time. I also take the time to write down answered prayers, so I can refer back to the goodness of God and thank Him. Writing down answered prayers reminds me that God has done it before and will surely do it again.

Other times I write down a specific prayer for someone and then pray for them daily. Still other times I'm led to pray for a specific person, and at times these are people I barely know.

I definitely think we have been put on this earth to be prayer vessels for others. Through having the privilege to attend Bible studies, I have learned the believer's authority prayer. As believers, God has given us the authority to pray with boldness and faith. We don't need to wait for a big illness to pray for healing; we can use our prayer authority to pray for the common colds and headaches as well.

I encourage people to make their prayers bold and full of faith by using authoritative speech. I believe that God doesn't need our prayer, but He desires our prayer and to have a close relationship with each of us.

I've experienced moments when I was so hurt and broken that uttering a single word in prayer was difficult and painful. I didn't know where to start, because starting a prayer might actually mean I would need to face my despair and pain. In times such as these, a simple "Help" is all I could say.

God heard my cry and sent me His helper, the Holy Spirit. In John 14:26, Jesus tells us, *"But the Counselor, the Holy Spirit, whom the Father will send in my name, will teach you all things and remind you of everything I have told you."* The Holy Spirit is our helper, counsellor, and strength. The Holy Spirit has been sent to represent Jesus and act on His behalf. He will remind us of all the promises in His Word. In any situation you find yourself in, you can trust and turn to your helper, the Holy Spirit, and ask Him for guidance in your time of need.

For me, prayer has many purposes. Some prayers are for confession and forgiveness, some are for protection, while others are meant to heal and help in times of trouble and despair. Don't be afraid to go to God in prayer, even if you feel as though it's been too long since your last conversation with God. The thing about God is that He is so loving and full of grace that He doesn't keep records of wrongs. He receives us with open arms, always ready for His children when they go to Him in prayer.

As Psalm 102:1 says, *"Lord, hear my prayer; let my cry for help come before you."* Asking God for help is a start. I believe that we aren't meant to face our hardships alone. He is our Father, and as a father He wants to help us.

Another prayer is one for the afflicted, when a person is overwhelmed and faint and pours out their complaint to God. I think many can relate to such a prayer, of feeling overwhelmed and not knowing where to turn.

Another key point in prayer is thankfulness and gratitude. As we read in Psalm 69:30, *"I will praise God's name with song and exalt him with thanksgiving."* Just as we are taught to say thank you from a very early age, we should thank God in prayer. Take the time each and every morning and evening to give thanks. Offering a simple thank you to God the minute we open our eyes is a good way to start the day, and saying it right before bed is a good way to go to sleep at night.

One particular scripture strikes me, from Philippians 4:6, *"Don't worry about anything, but in everything, through prayer and petition with thanksgiving, present your request to God."* These words tell us not to have anxiety.

Millions of people in the world suffer from some form of anxiety. This scripture tells us that in every situation—not just one or two or three, but all—we must be thankful to God, even when we're going through our darkest, loneliest times in life.

Finally, the verse tells us to present our requests to God. Well, that's specific enough: just tell God what it is you need. Is it healing? Is it clarity? Is it forgiveness? Is it motivation? Is it peace? Whatever it is, bring it to God in prayer.

In Matthew 18:19, Jesus says, *"Again, truly I tell you, if two of you on earth agree about any matter that you pray for, it will be done for you by my Father in heaven."* He's telling us to pray with one another, agree on the prayer request, and make it known to God. Then it will be done.

Another scripture I often hear comes from 1 Thessalonians 5:17, which simply says, *"Pray without ceasing"* (KJV). This scripture was written by the apostle Paul in one of his letters to the Thessalonians.

I've read this verse a number of times and heard it preached very often. But I've never experienced it like I have recently. Now I know the true meaning of praying without ceasing. Does this mean to pray nonstop? No! It actually means to go about our day with intervals of recurring prayer.

And yet, with our daily demands and constant hustles, can we always stop to kneel down to pray? My guess is that most of you would answer no. But our Father doesn't want a forced prayer; He longs for a relationship, communication, a heart of gratitude, and thanksgiving.

The important thing to remember is that we can pray anywhere and everywhere. While driving on our way to our work, while attending to our child's activities, while making meals, and while waiting at appointments… you get it, right?

However, praying without ceasing doesn't replace your alone time with God. We have been created to have alone time with our Creator. He has a desire for our attention and intimate time.

Human relationships require us to spend intimate time with one another, and the same is true of our relationship with God. In order to make it strong, powerful, secure, and unshakeable, we need time alone with God.

How can we spend time alone with God through all our daily demands? It takes discipline to set aside time each day to be with God. Avoid distractions and noise. If you're an early riser, one way is to spend time with God early in the morning. Whatever your schedule, be alert and find the time necessary to be with God.

Some might not know how to do this, but I encourage you to just set the time apart and the rest will come naturally.

Once your time is set, learn to expect. Expect God to teach you through His Word. Expect God to confirm His Word to you. Expect God to meet you in His presence.

Now, take His words and bring it to life by reading His promises. Take the time to study the Word of God, to study the Bible. And if you don't understand a passage, research it. Even if you take one passage per day, and fully understand it, it is better than reading a whole chapter and not understanding it at all. Once you've read a passage, pray about it. Meditate on what you've just read and ask God if there's any way it can be applied to your daily life.

Finally, make prayer a central part of your life.

Prayer gives us an opportunity to spend time with God, and spending time talking with Him through a daily prayer routine helps us to develop a deeper relationship with Him. Only then can we truly understand God's love and desire for each one of us.

Growing up in a Christian home, I knew who God was. I knew He loved me. I knew He had sent His Son Jesus to die for me. I knew the importance of believing in God. I knew the Bible stories. I knew how to pray. And I definitely knew the fear of God.

But if you were to ask me about my true prayer relationship with God as a teen, I'd be lying if I said I had a good one. I prayed, but did I really wait to hear back? No. I prayed and moved forward with my day. Most days, things went in my favour—and when they didn't, my prayers got longer and louder. But still I never waited. I never stopped to be still and listen.

I knew Psalm 46:10 and had it memorized: *"Be still, and know that I am God…"* (KJV) But I didn't practice it. I was convinced that I didn't know how to be still.

By nature, I am not a still person. I don't even like to be still when getting a therapeutic massage. Truth be told, I think I've been afraid of hearing any response from God—afraid of hearing what I couldn't control. What if God's answer wasn't the same as my answer? What if God wanted me to do this instead of that? Or worse, what if God didn't even hear me? I think I was more afraid of praying and not hearing from God than hearing what God actually had to say to me.

I have been married for over a decade, and most of my memories are good ones. However, I can admit that there have been challenging times in my marriage. My husband and I have faced times when we held tightly to our own points of view, neither wanting to give in. We didn't always see eye to eye and this caused friction, disagreements, arguments, and phases of silence between us.

At the beginning of my *in between* journey, our relationship wasn't at its best; our arguments increased and our respect for each other decreased. Apologies between us were far and few between, and it felt as though our marriage was headed towards destruction.

When I first told my husband about taking a leave of absence from work, he was supportive. But he was also confused and worried, along with many other emotions. Our conversations led to a lot of disagreement. He was afraid that I was leaving a career and consistent salary without knowing what the future held.

Our silence left me unsettled and sad, but I was faithful in the knowledge that God had bigger plans.

One afternoon when the kids were off to school and my husband was away on a business trip, I sat all alone in my living room in silence, preparing myself to read some scripture and pray. I felt tired and overwhelmed by loneliness and sadness.

I didn't know where to start, so I just fell to my knees in anguish. This wasn't just a prayer; it was a plea, a desperate cry for help. I didn't plea for physical help, though. What I needed was an intercession from God to speak to my husband and show him that his wife needed our marriage vows to be put into action. The meaning of "in sickness and health" was being put to the test.

In my moment of despair, as tears flowed down my face, my prayer became stronger, louder, unstoppable, and unceasing.

Then the phone rang. Even though I felt unfit to take the call during prayer, I was prompted to answer. When I picked up the phone, I heard the voice of my husband. He was sitting on a plane, preparing for takeoff on his return flight home.

But this time he sounded different; he was a different man. It was the man God had first given me, the husband he had promised to be.

"I'm sorry," he said. "I'm here for you."

There it was. In that moment, I realized that I was experiencing an answered prayer. I was experiencing what it meant to have said, "For better or worse." And in that moment, my faith grew and matured, increasing to another level.

The words I heard from my husband that day were a miracle. He went on to describe his love for me and his faith in our marriage. It was no less than a renewal of our vows and I lay down on the floor, in tears. From that moment, my husband's fear and uncertainty concerning our future switched to support and confidence that everything would be okay.

God has answered many prayers in my life. Another time, when my daughter was nine years old, she struggled with her sleep. Every night she was tormented by fear and anxiety and couldn't get her mind and body to calm down at bedtime. She would agonize and fight for hours before finally giving in to an unpeaceful rest.

She was at a breaking point and I couldn't just fix it by rocking her to sleep, as I had when she was a baby. However, as a mom I knew I had the power of prayer. I didn't know what else to do as her mom, but I wanted to fix her sleep-deprived body.

Once I understood that this was a supernatural battle, I gave it all to God. I prayed constantly when she woke up, right before she went to bed, and during the day when she was at school. I circled her room, and I believed! I knew God saw me and heard my plea.

That's when it happened. Healing came a few days into my prayer. It started with the first night of a restful sleep, and night after night after that our daughter had no more terror or anxiety.

Once again, I was reminded of God's grace and love.

For me, I know that God is great and that He answers all our hearts' desires, according to His will and His Word. What I mean by that is that we can't just go around asking things in prayer that go against what God wants for us or that go against what is written in His Word.

Before anyone is confused as to why some prayers aren't answered, we can ask ourselves some questions about what we've been requesting. Dissect the true meaning of your request. Is it selfless and aligned with God's Word, or is it a selfish request that doesn't come from a godly place?

Prayer is powerful, and once we study its power and put it into

*practice, we will never again live a
life of fear and what-ifs.*

Some people live each day without faith, waking up with fear and anxiety before they even face the day. What if we, for even just one day, woke up with the exact opposite emotion? What if we woke up and took on the day without any worries or fears?

I don't mean that we shouldn't worry because we have no responsibilities. Absolutely not. I mean that we should wake up and decide for the day that fear won't cripple us from making decisions. Anxieties won't creep up on us. For this one day, we'll be full of faith and have the courage to face the day that's been given to us.

Why is it that some people don't seem able to be fearless? Well, for the most part it's mindset. We've been conditioned to believe a certain way. These beliefs are portrayed for us in child-hood so that we don't know any other way of living. We think that by worrying we're being proactive, that the worry actually fixes the problem. As humans, we're compelled to feel that in order to fix a problem we have to dwell on it, even if all that negative thinking makes it worse.

In Matthew 6:27, Jesus asks, *"Can any of you add one moment to his life span by worrying?"* He asks this question knowing that we would end up worrying anyway.

Let me ask you a question: has it ever helped you to worry? It says right there in His Word that it does no good.

Sometimes we use prayer as a last resort rather than a first response. I truly believe that if we would make prayer a first re-sponse, a first priority, it would make a difference. I challenge you to go into prayer for any situation you're facing and give it to God.

Try it. You'll see the power of this approach. It will give you new meaning in life. Your faith will grow to new heights. Changes will happen. Some might notice them right away while others will look back and realize it after the fact.

I believe that life is meant to be enjoyed. I believe that it is our choice, our mindset, that allows us to either experience life as a joyful or unjoyful event.

Another truth about prayer is that sometimes God's response is loud and clear and given to us instantly, either through His Word, through a moment of worship, or through an actual person.

Other times the answer comes to us in a whisper. For me, it was a constant nagging voice in my sleep. It woke me up one day and I just had to get my Bible and read the verse I'd been hearing in my sleep: *"Blessed are the poor in spirt, for the kingdom of heaven is theirs"* (Matthew 5:3). What did this mean and why on earth was I being woken up about this?

One thing I've learned is that God speaks when I am still, and there is nothing more still than being in a state of sleep. In this state, my mind is most relaxed and uncluttered.

That morning, I decided to dig deep into the meaning of Matthew 5:3 and really understand what it was saying to me.

As I looked at the rest of the chapter, I started to feel amazed. These words, given to us by Jesus when He was on the earth, actually imparted eight blessings. We are so blessed to have these blessings recounted to us today, for Jesus Himself is telling us how we are to live.

These words that Jesus preached are known as the Beatitudes. When we choose to apply His words to our daily life, we'll notice that we can achieve a better quality of life here on earth.

Let us take a look at each beatitude, and along the way I will show you how I incorporate each one into my daily life.

1. *"Blessed are the poor in spirit, for the kingdom of heaven is theirs"* (Matthew 5:3). For me, this simply

means being satisfied with what I have and sharing the good things I have with others.

2. *"Blessed are those who mourn, for they will be comforted"* (Matthew 5:4). In other words, I am to comfort those who are suffering. I am to help others feel better about themselves after suffering loss.

3. *"Blessed are the humble, for they will inherit the earth"* (Matthew 5:5). I choose to be humble and truly not let my pride and ego get in my way. When I do something good, I do it for God and for His recognition, not for others. I don't boast or seek attention in doing good.

4. *"Blessed are they who hunger and thirst for righteousness, for they will be filled"* (Matthew 5:6). For me, this is simple: God is telling me to do what is fair and right according to His Word. I try to live free from sin.

5. *"Blessed are the merciful, for they will be shown mercy"* (Matthew 5:7). For me, this means that I am to offer forgiveness to those who are unkind to me. This is a hard one, but through forgiveness I show mercy, and in return God promises that I will be shown mercy. I choose to give mercy in order to get it in return.

6. *"Blessed are the pure in heart, for they will see God"* (Matthew 5:8). This verse strikes to my heart and really gets my attention. When my heart is clean and renewed, free from anger, hatred, and jealousy, and when I do God's will, it's as though I am seeing God through righteousness. It reminds me to have a heart like a child, pure.

7. *"Blessed are the peacemakers, for they will be called sons of God"* (Matthew 5:9). I try to bring peace in

this world, even though I'm only one person. I believe one person can make a difference. I try to control my behaviour in order to show the world peace and light and that Jesus lives in me.

8. *"Blessed are they who are persecuted because of righteousness, for the kingdom of heaven is theirs"* (Matthew 5:10). For me, this means that in everything I do, and in everything I'm faced with, I need to be willing to stand up for God's truth, even if that means being teased, insulted, and persecuted.

At many times in my life, I've been alone in my views. But I always stand my ground and stand up for my truth, and I will always continue to do so. My truth won't change just because others believe something else. I stand by God's Word, which has been standing from the beginning of time and hasn't changed.

These teachings on the Beatitudes leave me feeling satisfied, knowing that God tells me what behaviours and character He wants me to embody. The message still benefits us today, thousands of years later. It remains true and modern.

As I close this chapter, I hope that in some way you've found a new view on prayer. I hope that with each day you are given can start with a simple prayer of thanks to God the Father.

Three

MUSIC

MUSIC HAS SUCH A STRONG INFLUENCE ON ME. IT CAN CHANGE MY mood in an instant.

Many researchers have pondered the therapeutic benefits of music, and there are music therapy programs that are designed to help achieve goals, such as managing stress, enhancing memory, and alleviating pain.

Nicole C. Mullen has a song by the title "I Know My Redeemer Lives." For me, not only is this song powerful but the message is encouraging and inspiring. When I listen to this song, I am reassured that God is there for the weary and broken.

The Bible says in Philippians 4:19, *"And my God will supply all your needs according to his riches in glory in Christ Jesus."* This passage was written by the apostle Paul, and in it he encourages us by emphasizing that God will meet our needs. Our wants and needs are two very different things, though, and God knows our needs and provides accordingly.

Among the needs all people require are hope and security. In Mullen's song, I find the answer to my longing and hope. My hope rests in the One who created it all. By stopping to listen to this music, I can experience pure peace and joy, even for a moment in my chaotic day.

A wise woman once told me that our greatest weapon against the enemy is to worship in the form of music. So when I feel defeated, when I'm at my lowest and feeling run down, I take my weapon of music and fight through praise music.

To praise God is to express our adoration for Him. I praise and glorify His name. I give God honour, high respect and great esteem, even in the middle of whatever storm I face.

I choose to listen to music daily, especially worship music. And I'm continually amazed at how I feel; it always seems as though the songs are meant specifically for me.

When I listen to music, the lyrics pour out like rain, each word echoing healing, restoration, and hope.

During my *in between* journey, I longed for hope, for the day when I'd finally find myself again. Some days I didn't know what else to do, but I knew that worship and music would give me peace. When the music plays, no one and nothing can take my peace from me.

When I face periods of my life when I can't utter a single word in prayer, I lift up my voice in praise because I know that God hears! I feel surrounded by His love and goodness.

Another powerful song that resonates with me is "Surround-ed" by Michael W. Smith. We have been given the power to speak and sing and use our voices. The voice is a powerful weapon and using it in times when we feel most defeated is so powerful.

I have sometimes found myself fighting many different types of battles, some physical, others mental, and still others emotional. During the battles, it may feel like I'm surrounded by sadness, anxiety, worry, and pain, but when I use my voice to worship and praise, I am given help for the fight.

Another powerful worship song is "Goodness of God" by Bethel Music and Jenn Johnson. When I listen to it, I remember all the good things I've experienced. I forget my hurt, pain, and sadness and am filled with goodness.

Each of us has experienced goodness at one time or another, before life became a series of routines and responsibilities. I encourage you to dig deep and find those memories. Write them down. Remember when you felt most grateful and were filled with God's faithfulness and goodness.

I find that taking time alone to be in full thankfulness and worship with God is powerful. I cannot begin to express the peace and truth that have come out of my worship sessions. In them, I'm reminded of God's promises and His miracles. I'm encouraged to continue pressing forward, reminded that fear and unbelief are just ways of distracting me from my true purpose.

Some are sceptical and think that people only worship and sing praise when things are all right in their lives, but I can tell you, as I sit here and type these words, that I am currently *in between*. I am conquering each and every day. I'm fighting. I'm not giving up. I'm choosing to move forward with the purpose that has been revealed to me. I'm choosing not to back down. I'm choosing not to be afraid. I'm choosing to stand in faith and believe that what God has asked me to do is exactly what I need to be doing.

I'm experiencing the middle of the storm. To be honest, this is the best place I've been so far. If being in the middle of the storm feels this good while I worship, I most certainly can't wait to worship when the sun is out and the storm has passed.

As I've allowed the *in between* stage to manifest, I've begun to enjoy the journey. Along the way I've met some extraordinary women, all whom are strong and courageous yet somehow broken, hurt, tired, and worn down. Some of these women I'd never met and were introduced to me by a friend or acquaintance. Others I've known all my life and have only now taken the opportunity to explore with them.

The one thing we all have in common is that we love and in return need to be loved. We need to be heard and understood. We know that we need one another so we can help others outside of our circle. We are the women *in between*, the ones who are learning to love, laugh, and live. We know the importance of treating ourselves well, so that in return we can pass down to our children the confidence and tools they can use to cope and enjoy their own journeys.

Four
BOUNDARIES

THESE TWO WORDS, LIMITS AND BOUNDARIES, ARE SO POWERFUL— and once put into action, they can have a big impact on your future.

There were many times in my career when I didn't set proper limits and boundaries. I found myself constantly complying and agreeing to unrealistic deadlines and demands. I was so afraid to get in trouble, afraid of being seen as a rebel, that I chose to stay quiet instead.

On one occasion at my job, while my husband was out of town on a work trip, I chose to work later than usual, knowing that I wouldn't make it in time to pick up the children from school at the bus stop that day. I made this choice because I was afraid to set a limit with my employer. It was my responsibility to get my children at a certain time, yet I was so boundaryless that I missed their pickup time. As soon as I got in the car after work, I became stuck in traffic. Sweating from worry and panic, I scrambled through my phone, calling family and friends to see if anyone would be able to get to the bus stop when my children got off the bus.

Through this, I learned the real meaning of setting limits. I was driven to the point of setting boundaries, and probably making some enemies along the way, because I hadn't ever practiced how to do it correctly.

I didn't set boundaries because I felt too ashamed. I was afraid of being unloved, judged, or viewed the wrong way. Whatever it was I felt, I eventually learned that setting limits and keeping healthy boundaries equalled *freedom*. Freedom from the imaginary chains I had created from years of lacking boundaries. Freedom from worrying about what others thought of me.

The truth is that I have absolutely no control over someone else's thoughts. Whether they express their feelings about me out loud or I make assumptions about how they feel in my own head, I can't actually change anything. So in my experience, the best thing to do is set boundaries in order to form healthier friendships and relationships.

Trying to bottle up my emotions and get it all inside meant that I never said no. I had a "superwoman complex," as someone once told me—and this someone was the very person I failed to set a boundary with. I was constantly taking on responsibilities, especially at work, that didn't belong to me. This led me to a very unhealthy mindset which took me quite some time to undo.

My trusted counsellor introduced me to a book, *Boundaries*, by author Dr. Henry Cloud and Dr. John Townsend. This book has been an asset and very important tool in my *in between* journey. It has both taught me about myself and helped me to recognize when I'm in a situation where there's a need to set a clear and healthy boundary.

I've learned how to set limits using proper words and tones.

Setting boundaries has helped me develop a better perspective and allowed me to be alert at all times.

My first step was recognizing and admitting who I was and recognizing my compliant attitude. I felt inclined to obey rules and agree with others. I often found myself saying yes to others without thinking twice about whether I could actually follow through. I took on projects and deadlines at work that led to suppressed stress and anxieties. I was highly accommodating and always cooperative.

It took years, but I finally realized that that kind of attitude leads to burnout.

My second step was to set healthy boundaries. Since this is an area I wasn't very familiar with, I started with simple things, such as saying no to getting a cup of coffee with a friend on a night when I felt tired and exhausted.

I learned how to listen to my own body when it told me, *That isn't an activity you can handle right now.* Only once I was able to recognize my body's triggers could I set limits and obey that voice inside me.

I felt liberated and confident. When I stopped creating their response in my mind, I was set free. I often judged what they were thinking, imagining the way conversations would take place, and this produced such an unhealthy mindset.

I learned that no one has the right to take my limits and boundaries from me. They are mine to set and mine to follow through on.

I decided to take this opportunity to spend time with myself, learn about me, and make me healthier, both in mind and body.

I learned how to respond instead of react to others' comments. Let me repeat that again: I learned to respond and not react. This is so important, because reacting to people is what caused me to try controlling situations through anger, yelling, and rash words. By instead choosing to respond, I noticed my feelings and was able to take a pause, a breath, and consider my response to the situation.

I cannot express how important this very simple change has been in terms of impacting my life. After many failed attempts at reacting instead of responding, I can finally say that I'm really getting it. I'm finally enjoying the freedom that comes from not having so many unnecessary arguments.

This boundary—choosing to respond instead of react—has made such a big difference. And by having children of my own, I have also realized that it's very important for children to learn this at a very young age. I've noticed that children sometimes react to situations with anger and bitterness. My own children turn to having battles with each other all because they sometimes choose to react to one another's annoying tactics instead of properly responding.

Responding instead of reacting isn't the easiest skill to acquire. However, once my husband and I began demonstrating this strategy to our children, we were able to give them the ability to choose to respond instead of reacting. Children will be faced with far more challenging situations as they get older, so instilling healthy boundaries at a young age will leave them well prepared.

I took the time to pray and ask God for the wisdom to properly and respectfully answer others. Funnily enough, once I asked God for this, I immediately started to find myself in situations that made me set limits. It varied from simple things, like my children's chores being ignored or limiting their amount of screen time, to saying no to friends and family for things big and small. I somehow found myself setting many limits and it sure felt good.

In the beginning, I felt slightly uncomfortable, emotionally, but as time went on and I set more boundaries and limits, I felt less uncomfortable. The discomfort shifted from me to the other person. I felt almost sad for them when they spoke to me in a certain tone, like they expected something from me that I couldn't give them.

I took the time to research why others demanded things from me, and through that I learned many characteristics about others. Although I wish that everyone would want to explore and improve their own characters, I learned that it isn't my responsibility. Instead of dwelling on someone's else character, I choose to improve mine as best I can.

Oftentimes at work, I found myself complying with others and saying yes to unrealistic deadlines, as though I wanted them to realize how well I listened. I realize now that behaving this way left me completely drained and unhappy.

Not setting any boundaries led me to explore and discover reasons as to why I had developed the mindset of always saying yes and doing more than I could handle in the first place.

I remind myself that setting boundaries is not a one-time event; it's a daily practice in my life now. Because of this newly developed mindset, I have found freedom from many situations.

I have to admit that it feels good to finally use my voice to set limits that are designed to protect me. I'm amazed at how we can use our voice. Some take it for granted, but when we look at it carefully, we see that our words and expressions are all brought to life with our voice.

When I look at what God's Word has to say about words and about our voice, it is clear that God is telling us to choose our words wisely. Proverbs 18:21 tells us, *"Death and life are in the power of the tongue..."* I interpret this to mean that our words have the power to either bless or curse others. We should be attentive to how we choose to use our words. With our words, we can either build someone up or tear them down.

When my child comes home after school and presents me with their assignment, I can either choose to uplift their effort or tear them down and demand better. Which one do you think my child will cherish more? If I want to teach them that their voice is powerful, a good way to show them would be to use my voice to lift them up instead of tearing them down.

I have learned, and continue to learn, about boundaries in different areas of my life. I've come to recognize the need to set boundaries at work and at home, and with my children, friends, and family… even with myself.

When I think about my children, my goal is to help them to survive on their own. There are different parenting stages, and once my child is of a certain age I begin to shift from a more controlling style of parenting to an influencing style. Control parenting is when I have to tell my children what to do and influence parenting is when my actions speak louder than my words.

My goal is that my children, when they reach the proper age, will no longer need me to tell them what to do next—for example, to do their chores, homework, eating, etc. Rather they will have been properly influenced by my actions and have the ability to do these tasks all on their own.

My role as a parent changes as my children grow. Their needs change and their minds develop. So the way I parent them as children will be different to how I parent them as tweens, teens, and young adults.

As a baby, my child needs constant care, feeding, changing, holding, bathing, and sleeping. This changes once they're toddlers. At this stage, they have the ability to play on their own, use utensils to feed themselves, use the potty independently, stay in the bath alone but supervised, and have a simpler bedtime routine.

As a child, they become more independent and are given more limits and boundaries. When playing, the child becomes responsible for clean-up after playtime. Their bedtime routine becomes stricter and they need to have better table manners and greater responsibilities, such as setting and unsetting the table for breakfast, lunch, and dinner.

As tweens, they should know their limits in several areas, such as with screen time, friend time, and leisure time. A tween is given more freedom as trust is built.

And finally, by the time they're teens we are likely into the influence parenting phase. By this age, they know how to set their own limits, schedule their own routines, and take care of their responsibilities.

I constantly pray about teaching my children properly, and I take time to learn in order to teach my children boundaries at a young age. I say no when necessary and set healthy limits and responsibilities and expectations so they can grow up to be healthy, well-spoken adults.

Five

RUTH

WHEN SOMEONE IS DIAGNOSED WITH AN ILLNESS, IT'S NATURAL that they want to fight it to get well. A person usually goes to the doctor and then takes the medication prescribed to them.

But for some reason, when a person is diagnosed with a head problem, as I like to call it, they act differently. At least, that's how it was for me. Guilt set in, and an array of emotions overtook me. I believed that a non-physical condition didn't need to be treated. The people around me, the ones I loved most, didn't see me in physical pain, so they seemed to diminish my emotional pain, which in turn made me feel inadequate and guilty.

The cure to a head problem for me was to believe that I could overcome it and have the courage to face it head-on and fight. It can be a different kind of fight than for a physical problem, but the main idea is to fight. Fight by seeking help. Fight by seeking guidance.

Therapy was a fantastic way for me to learn about myself and what was going on in my head. I also fought by learning and reading. Learning is knowledge, knowledge is wisdom, and of course wisdom is power. Wisdom is the quality of having good judgment, intelligence, understanding, perceptiveness, and discernment.

I also fought by reaching out, since I believe we aren't meant to handle these sorts of problems on our own.

In this chapter, I won't tell you about the typical lying-down-on-a-couch kind of therapy, so to speak. But I will discuss the counselling sessions I've experienced during my *in between* journey.

I remember my first call to Ruth like it was yesterday. She was a highly recommended counsellor, and after making the appointment I could hardly wait the next few weeks before getting the chance to meet her. I felt as though I needed her right away but knew I had to be patient.

During the drive to her office, I was nervous, anxious, and a little happy, as if she would have all the answers I'd been longing for. I thought she might have the cure.

I arrived a few minutes early and made my way to the waiting room. It was warm, inviting, and had character. This wasn't a cold, uninviting office setting.

Ruth soon came out to greet me and led me to one of the empty counselling rooms. Once there, I sat in a rustic but comfortable chair and our conversation began.

I was an emotional wreck in that first session, to be honest. I was scared, emotionally and physically burned out, and full of anxiety and despair. But I was also hopeful. I knew the instant I left her office that day that this was going to be the beginning of something great.

Ruth is now my one and only go-to therapist. Along the way, I've come to consider her a mentor and friend, a confidant and advisor.

Every session started with prayer, which set the tone for peace and truth to follow. Ruth didn't push prayer on me, but rather she asked in her gentle voice if we could start the sessions that way. I accepted, and afterward every session started with Ruth dedicating the session to God and in return asking God to bless our words and open our mouths, ears, eyes, and heart to healing.

Her wisdom took me to places I never even knew existed. I visited childhood memories, some happy ones, some sad, and some angry. I never expected to open pages I had already turned and closed. I didn't want to revisit some of those memories that I had hidden deep within my mind. These memories had made such an impact on me, making me feel stuck the way I was.

But in each session a page was opened and read out loud for me to hear, not the thirty-nine-year-old me but the girl I used to be. Ruth showed me how to take that girl and hold her if she needed to be held, to cry with her if she needed to cry, to laugh with her if she needed to laugh, and pray with her if she needed to pray.

Most of all, we healed her. We spoke to her with a tender and gentle voice. We listened to her. We didn't silence her, but instead nurtured and welcomed her.

Ruth taught me the importance of my voice. She showed me how to speak and not shut out the words. She showed me that my words need to be heard. When a situation arose, she taught me how to respond and not react.

She also taught me that my voice has the power to literally give life to something or put it to death. I now choose to give life to my words, and I choose to do this so I can to pass this down to my children and their children.

Ruth taught me so many things. She showed me that I don't need others' approval, that I am enough, that God values me, and that my work is valuable. She showed me that my destiny is too great for me to be distracted by people who are never going to affirm me. She showed me that when God leads me to do something, He will energize me to fulfill the call.

From this, I learned that the work I chose to do once I was able to return would never leave me drained and emotionally burned out again. I trusted that God would lead me to do work that will keep me growing and keep me healthy.

As the months progressed, my sessions with Ruth slowly diminished. The weekly sessions became monthly, and eventually only every six months. After that, they became sporadic, or even just emails when I needed a quick encouraging word.

Ruth's guidance and knowledge made me feel powerful and confident. Her words always helped me find the answer inside, and she had an incredible way of allowing me to find it. Every time a situation arose, Ruth broke it down just enough so I could start unravelling the truth behind it and eventually see the solution. Most of the time, the solution required consistent work, but this never bothered me; I wanted the work because I knew it would lead me to progress and success.

I have now been given the tools I need to take any situation I'm faced with and bring it to light and speak truth.

During my sessions, I also learned gifts about myself that I never knew I could use. I had passions and enjoyed doing many things, I hadn't realized that God gives each and every one of us a gift.

In Romans 12:6, the apostle Paul says, *"According to the grace given to us, we have different gifts…"* The next few verses go on to name each gift:

If prophecy, use it according to the proportion of one's faith; if service, use it in service; if teaching, in teaching; if exhorting, in exhortation; giving, with generosity; leading, with diligence; showing mercy, with cheerfulness. (Romans 12:6–8)

I once shared with Ruth a passion of mine. At first I was slightly embarrassed, because I had never expressed this passion with anyone, but the whole point of going to these sessions was to get things off my mind and out of my mouth.

I took the chance and told her that I liked to write. I had started writing this book—or at least, a few chapters of it—and while writing I felt as though this was where I wanted to be. When I write, I feel most comfortable and at ease. At that time I didn't even know that I knew how to write or express myself, but when I was writing I was in my element, filled with passion.

I continued with my writing and had Ruth read a few chapters. I wanted her feedback and opinion. What I got in return was a word that made me realize my gift. The word she used to describe me was "teacher." Interestingly, I had always wanted to be a teacher when I was younger, but I hadn't pursued it. Now I realize that being a teacher comes in many forms. I have become a teacher to my children as well as to my readers—and also in my new career.

I also realized that the gifts mentioned in the Bible include being a teacher. I am grateful to have discovered my gift, and I'm even more grateful to be using it. I am always amazed at the Word of God and all His teachings. When I read His Word, I discover answers for every situation I find myself in.

Another teaching I received from Ruth had to do with consistency and mindset.

I learned that I have power over my thoughts, and creating awareness is one of the ways in which I can remain consistent.

For me, having a morning routine required consistent work and mental stimulation. Every morning when I get up, I push myself to start off the day positively through thankful prayer, doing devotions, journaling, and making mental choices to make the day good and productive. These routines help prevent me from getting stuck *in between* again. Some days are more difficult than others, but I remind myself of who I am—and whose I am. With that confidence, I can start the day on a positive footing.

I am so grateful for all that I've been given. And most of all I'm grateful that my moments of feeling stuck no longer last longer than a few minutes, hours, or a few days. This is much better than feeling that way for weeks and months. If I start feeling stuck, I encourage myself to change my mindset from negative to positive.

I remember Ruth's voice from time to time, especially in moments when I find myself transported back to helplessness, solitude, and complete and utter despair, I hear her lessons being repeated in my mind and remember the actions to take next.

Ruth didn't magically turn my situation into a fairy tale, but she took a young, helpless girl and instilled in her hope—a hope I want to share with anyone I can. She opened doors of confidence, truth, and love. I am still learning and discovering all these new paths, but I can truly say that I have also learned from Ruth to never stop learning.

When I don't have the answer to a situation, I've learned to take a step back and pray, explore, discover, and research. Eventually the right solution does come up.

Some days I look back and recall the girl who first walked into Ruth's office on that cold February morning, and I'm grateful for the transformation I experienced, developing into a confident, unstoppable, faithful woman.

If you can find your Ruth, I highly recommend it. But there is a difference between a therapist and what I had in Ruth. Her core characteristic is altruism. She truly roots for you to find happiness. She's rooted in love and grace and her goal is for you to find and discover yourself through God's eyes.

I am thankful for each and every session, thankful that Ruth opened up my mind to explore past experiences and allow forgiveness, love, and hope to shine through with each and every discovery. I'm grateful that Ruth was always consistent in her teachings and understanding with me, and grateful that she never pushed her opinions on me, instead only sharing truth and love from the very beginning.

I am forever grateful to have been placed in her path.

Six

JOY

I MET JOY ONE YEAR INTO MY *IN BETWEEN* JOURNEY. JOY IS A BUBBLY young woman with an undamaged enthusiasm and optimistic character. Her laugh is contagious and her smile warm. When I first met her, I could tell she was driven by her genuine hope that I could succeed through my work with her.

Joy was my occupational therapist.

An occupational therapist is someone who helps people recover and improve their daily lives and ability to work. In my case, since I suffered severe burnout at work, her job was to help treat and guide me into the future.

When I walked into her office, I was greeted by the lady at the front desk and asked to complete some forms. I was sceptical at first, but once Joy came to greet me and lead me to her office, her warm smile and kind energy made me feel comfortable and allowed me to embrace the experience.

The office we sat in was welcoming yet a little cold and dull. It had chairs that reminded me of the ones I would find in a waiting room. A desk separated us. There were also large windows with a view of the road outside.

In some ways, I felt like a mother figure to this young woman. Joy was younger than I was and had newly gotten engaged a few months before. We hit it off immediately, and during our first session she spoke of her dazzling engagement ring and bewildering proposal in Europe. Her eyes blazed with innocent love and devotion to the married life ahead of her.

I often wondered what on earth Joy could bring to the table for me. Who was she? Why was I in her office explaining for the thousandth time why I felt burned out? At first I felt like she wasn't helping me at all; I just felt annoyed that I had to drive to her for weekly sessions.

I did, however, learn plenty from Joy. She taught me how to challenge myself and not be afraid doing it. She introduced the thought of there being a creative side to me. She showed me a list of activities—physical activities, manual activities, intellectual activities, relaxing activities and social activities— and together we reviewed each item and spoke about what I'd like to do.

We spent the first session analyzing these activities and choosing the ones I liked. She told me not to think too much about it; if I liked the activity, I should simply check it off. It didn't have to be something I'd already done.

And so I began to check items off the list.

At first it wasn't easy for me to go through such a list at my age and at this point in my life. I felt as though I didn't even know what I wanted to do. I had literally been the caretaker for my family for the past ten years and had almost forgotten what it was like to do anything for myself.

Although I was reluctant at first, I accepted this task and reviewed the form with Joy. We went over each activity. Some brought back dear childhood memories, the freedom of playing outdoors with my family, and simply reading and writing alone in my room as a child.

The list reminded me of important values I still carry with me today.

I was remembering who I was and who I wanted to be, finally becoming hopeful for what the future could offer if I just took a leap of faith and eliminated the fear that constantly crept up on me.

I learned to find my own joy in activities. I explored, researched, and found that girl, the one I had forgotten, the one who had dreams and hopes, and I made her happy.

I started out by adopting the puppy I had always wanted. I took the puppy for walks, which kept me busy and allowed me to focus on something other than my fears and anxieties.

I took long, relaxing baths without the guilt of someone needing me, which amazingly helped to ease the pain in my aching bones. I checked in with my doctor through regular appointments and counselling sessions and kept my mind healthy and strong. I fed myself healthy meals and even went to the gym. I met special friends along the way, and they accompanied and encouraged me through some of these activities. I created bonds with other women and shared conversations with them.

I encouraged myself and showed myself that it's okay to be confident. Most importantly, I learned to love myself. I listened to myself when I needed to rest, and I listened to myself when I needed to communicate with loved ones. I didn't silence myself any longer. I gave myself a voice and I made myself know that it needed to be heard.

I took what I learned from Joy and started to nurture the young child inside me.

Joy also introduced me to ways in which I could apply limits and boundaries. She taught me that even when we verbally express our limits, sometimes the other person doesn't hear them. I started to remember many instances when I had tried to voice limits at work and in return gotten no acknowledgement. This eventually left me frustrated and tired.

Joy explained that in cases where the other person didn't hear my limit, I had to choose how to react. In other words, I could choose to stop the person when it happened and restate my limit. I realize now that I didn't do that when it happened to me, because I wasn't assertive. Instead I chose to be silenced.

I left her office wondering why I wasn't assertive enough. Somewhere along the way I had learned to allow other people's voices to be stronger and louder than mine—not loud in an obnoxious way, but loud enough that the other person didn't physically hear me.

In that session, I realized that I would no longer allow that to happen. I assured myself that I was valued and my voice mattered. And as I continued to research boundaries and limits, I implemented many healthy boundaries in my life.

I allowed myself to open up to Joy. I took the shame that was buried deep within me and let it out. I voiced it and brought it to light, and once I did that I felt the shame and guilt depart.

I learned that I'm not responsible for other people's actions, nor am I responsible for their feelings towards the limits I have put in place.

These sessions with Joy were some of my hardest sessions. They opened my eyes to the choices I had made and showed me the consequences of my past decisions. But they also made me promise to work and improve myself and never again allow anyone to take my voice from me.

I learned the importance of my voice being heard and understood. I learned how to communicate clearly so my words would be understood the second time, if they weren't heard the first time. I also learned to judge situations well yet be sensitive, well-spoken, and assertive.

I used to think being assertive meant people would hate me. This fear held me back from setting limits and boundaries, but with proper research I learned that being assertive is a core communication skill. It means that I can express myself effectively and stand up for what I believe in while also respecting the rights and beliefs of others.

I would no longer allow others to intimidate or bully me.

In my final sessions with Joy, our relationship grew. I could tell she was so proud of the work she had accomplished with me. And so was I. She was proud of the new journey I was embarking on just a few months after first walking into her office hopeless and in full despair.

We looked at new career options and what it would look like if I returned to my previous job. We ultimately chose to focus on a new and healthier career, and Joy helped in the decision-making process.

Never could I have imagined that I would get to that point after only a few months. I was full of dreams, out of despair, and no longer filled with anxiety. I was ready to fight fear and take on a whole new journey, not to mention a whole new career. A career I would have never imagined myself in.

But things were different this time. I no longer lived in fear. I no longer believed I wasn't good enough. I no longer allowed other people's manipulative behaviour determine my value and worth. This time I had tools, limits, and boundaries to help me on my journey.

Joy was young, but she was also skilled. She knew that moments of relapse would follow, so she prepared me for that. She gave me worksheets to take home which would impact my next moves. Whenever I found myself falling into a negative mindset, these worksheets helped reset my mindset.

The worksheet was divided into three parts: the healthy zone, the risk zone, and the relapse zone. The point of this worksheet is to help people recognize the signs of entering the risk zone, such as anxiety, burnout, and stress. When I find myself in that place, I need to get myself back into the healthy zone. By writing down what it means to be in the healthy zone, by identifying what the relapse zone looks like, I could name all my feelings and move myself to a healthier place.

Before meeting Joy, an exercise like this would have seemed ridiculous and unnecessary, but along my *in between* journey I have come to understand that faith, mindset, and perception are my most important tools to help me succeed and live a joyful, meaningful life.

On my last day with Joy, we worked on the worksheet together for practice. It wasn't easy, because I no longer felt like I was in a risk zone, and in order to complete the worksheet I had to go back in time and put myself in my unhealthiest point in order to write down on paper everything I had gone through, every sad and helpless emotion.

But it wasn't as difficult as I had imagined, because this time I was equipped with the proper tools to get out of the risk zone. I believed in myself and I had strategies to keep my mind healthy and free of toxic thoughts and patterns.

I am now able to recognize resentment, which for me had led to burnout. I speak to it and ask, "What am I doing that I shouldn't be doing?" When I find myself constantly thinking about the same repetitive situation, I take the time to ask myself certain questions in order to be open and honest with myself and release it to God.

I no longer hold on to untruthful thoughts. I set boundaries with myself. I take care of my own thoughts and speak truth in love to myself. I no longer linger with thoughts of how conversations should play out or thoughts about what another person is thinking.

I have finally realized that I can't control how others think. I only have control over my own thoughts.

One day as I was reading, I came across this verse. As James 1:2–4 says,

Consider it a great joy, my brothers and sisters, whenever you experience various trials, because you know that the testing of your faith produces endurance. And let endurance have its full effect, so that you may be mature and complete, lacking nothing.

I am grateful to have experienced trials and I am grateful to have met Joy and thankful that she reminded me of the joy I had been lacking in my own life.

Seven

PIANO

EVER SINCE I WAS A LITTLE GIRL, THE PIANO HAS INTRIGUED ME. I was fascinated by the sound that came from one's fingers tapping against the keys and became curious about how musicians created such wonder. Whenever I hear the piano being played, the sounds soothe me. It makes me feel calm, as though I'm wrapped up and protected.

As a child I always wanted to learn the piano. My parents caved to my tenacity and determination, and at the age of eight I started piano lessons. Sadly, that didn't last for more than two sessions. I gave up and dropped the lessons. It was just too hard.

I look back in regret and wish I hadn't given up. I wish someone had pushed me to pursue it longer, no matter how hard it felt at the time.

But my piano journey didn't end there. Thirty years later, as I sat in the waiting area of my daughter's music school, waiting an hour and a half for her weekly music lesson to end, I thought about taking piano lessons all over again. I mean, I was already accompanying my daughter to the school every week. Why not use the time wisely and take a lesson myself?

I told my husband and children about my idea to take a few lessons. Knowing of my love for the piano, they soon surprised me with a gift certificate for piano lessons. I cheerfully and excitedly embarked on the challenge. I attended each lesson like an enthusiastic child.

But once again, I must admit it was a lot more difficult than I had anticipated.

I learned the basics and was a proud beginner graduate. Yet I chose not to pursue it further. At this point in my life, I knew that taking on an unrealistic challenge would lead to disappointment. So instead of pushing my limits, I listened to the voice inside that congratulated me on this small but nonetheless important achievement.

I was content to have taken the time to do what I had always wanted to do. This allowed me to move forward and not get stuck in a moment in time. If I hadn't taken those piano lessons, I would have always imagined what it was like to play; the what-ifs would have crept in and created many lies. Instead I was able to feel happy and fulfilled. I am content today that I'm able to play the piano unprofessionally and just for the fun of it.

Once I completed the beginner's course, knowing that I didn't want to pursue it further, I still wanted to own a piano. I don't know if it was for the look of having a piano in my home or the thought that having a piano would bring comfort and feelings of completion.

All I knew is that I really wanted a piano. But I also knew that my husband wasn't interested in sharing this quite expensive piece of furniture with me. On many occasions I would slip the idea into conversation, letting him know exactly where I would place it in the family room.

I showed him photos whenever I found a local seller, and his reply was always no. With each no, I was devastated, but not broken. We had agreed early on in our marriage that big furniture purchases needed to be discussed and agreed upon in advance.

Still, something inside me didn't give up. I pushed the issue and brought it up over and over again. I prayed that he would open himself up to giving one small yes…

Then, one day, he said it: "If the piano is free, it could be possible."

I took these words and prayed even harder. I brought them to life and didn't give up. The door was open; I just had to find the way in.

But how? Even the free sellers online had expensive shipping fees. I knew that wouldn't work.

God has perfect timing and His ways and plans are always perfect.

So I left it in His hands and moved on. God had this, and I believed that in time the piano would come.

And then it happened, years later. When I was in the middle of my *in between* journey, when I was broken, it literally showed up.

On a hot, humid, exhausting August afternoon, my kids were playing and running around the yard. My eldest child had a friend over that afternoon and they were splashing around in the water, enjoying the last days of summer before going back to school.

As the afternoon came to an end, we all got into the car to drive my daughter's friend home.

And there it was—*the piano*—on the curb by a neighbour's front yard, with a paper taped to it that said "Giving away." I drove right past it at first, not reversing back until a few moments later when I realized what the note said.

I had to look twice. Why would someone give away a perfectly good piano? And how had someone not snatched this up already?

Feeling grateful, I said out loud, "Thank You, Lord."

As I searched for the homeowners, I saw that there was no one around. I had so many questions. How long had this piano been on the curb? Could I just take it away? Why had no one taken it yet? Was it reserved for someone?

I stared at it from my car seat and waited, deciding what to do next. Thoughts kept running through my mind. Was this piano really just being given away? At no cost? Free?

I remembered what my husband had said—that the only way to bring a piano into our home was if it didn't cost us anything.

In an instant, I did it. I chose to take the piano.

Okay, so I didn't physically take the piano then and there, because it weighed a ton and I had the children with me, but I did call my handyman neighbour and asked him to help me take it directly to my house.

But I didn't think it through. I knew the havoc and disagreement this would cause between my husband and me, but a part of me didn't care. All I knew was that I wanted the piano, and in that moment I did whatever I needed to do to get it home. Well, in the garage at least, as that was where I would do my restoring.

I smiled to myself as I thought about restoring the piano. I felt a sense of peace as I envisioned the nourishment and fulfillment I would get from taking on this project. I thought of the healing it would bring me.

Now, for those of you who are married, you might understand the importance of discussing with your spouse any plan to bring a big piece of furniture into the house, let alone a piano that needs to be cleaned, sanded down, and painted. I knew this wouldn't be an easy explanation, but I was prepared for it. I knew every angle of defence, every convincing point, how to cross-examine everything he said to me.

When he came home that evening and saw a piano sitting in the garage, he was speechless. What was this piano doing in our garage and how had it gotten there? I told him the whole story and he just listened without saying a word.

We didn't speak much about it because we were in a rush to get ready and leave for the evening, but he did ask the basics. Where? How? Why? He didn't believe my story at first. Once he took it all in, though, surprisingly he didn't get upset. He was amazed that God had provided me with the piano I had always wanted—and for free.

We went to my sister's house that evening and didn't speak about it again for a while. I was kind of happy that we ignored the subject. I was scared of what my family would think of me. I hoped once we got to visiting with my sister and her family that my husband would have forgotten about the whole thing.

But he hadn't. When the subject came up again, I found myself trying to convince my husband and the rest of my family that I wasn't crazy, just inspired.

Crazy is what it felt like, but as I spoke to them about wanting to do whatever it took to turn this old piano into pure beauty, it turned out that they supported me. No one, not even my husband, fought me over it. It's like they knew I needed this.

During this *in between* stage, I suffered many grey days, and this project was just what I needed to begin getting unstuck.

Thinking back on that evening, I'm so grateful for the support system I had. These people believe in me. I am forever grateful and blessed to have them in my life.

And so my piano project began. I had no idea how to restore furniture, let alone a piano, so I got myself to a hardware store, found a paint expert, and asked every question I could think of about refurbishing an old piano. To my surprise, it was quite simple. Not easy, not fast, but simple.

I began my work on the piano one day at a time and worked at it any chance I got. Every time I went into the garage to work, I put in my earbuds and listened to motivational speakers and music. With a lot of patience and perseverance, and many inspirational songs, eventually the piano was finished.

My next step was to figure out how to get the piano from the garage to the living room. It was very heavy and I didn't want any of my loved ones to hurt themselves trying to lift it. So I found a moving company that was able to come move the piano for a very reasonable price.

And now, sitting in my living room, is the white piano I always wanted.

I later returned to the neighbour who had originally put the piano on the curb to show her photos of what I had done. I had the pleasure to chat with her about the history of the piano. It had belonged to her grandmother and was passed down from one generation to the next. But she was moving in the next few months and needed to downsize; her children didn't want to keep the piano for themselves, so she had decided to give it away instead of throwing it out.

She was amazed by the photos I showed her, shocked at what the piano looked like now. She didn't even know me and yet she congratulated me on the outcome.

For me, restoring the piano was an accomplishment. It was my way of growing and learning. Each time I think about the process of refurbishing this piano, I realize that I was also in the process of refurbishing myself. With each paint stroke, my confidence increased, my shame melted away.

I believe we each have the ability to learn, explore, and find out who we really are inside. I encourage others to take that step and start the journey to the piano, whatever "the piano" is for you. For some it may be discovering your love of nature, or music, or writing. Whatever it may be, it's never too late to take that leap and start your *in between* project.

Eight
FAITH

WHAT IS FAITH? I'VE OFTEN ASKED MYSELF THIS QUESTION. IS FAITH really about believing something I haven't yet seen? Is faith really about believing in miracles? Is faith different for each person? Can people have different amounts of faith? Does faith define who we are? Are we created with faith, or is it something we're taught and then able to practice?

These are all questions I found myself asking during my *in between* journey.

Hebrews 11:1 says, *"Now faith is the reality of what is hoped for, the proof of what is not seen."* Faith means having complete confidence, trust, belief, conviction, dependence, and reliance in God. This type of faith is based on spiritual understanding rather than proof.

Growing up in a Christian household, this type of faith was normal for me. We would pray for just about anything and I would have faith that what I prayed for would turn out. When I felt ill as a child, I would turn to my mom, who would in turn lay her hand on me and pray, and I would just believe it would get better. I don't know if it was because my mom was so confident in her prayers or the fact that a few hours passed and eventually I would have felt better anyway, but I do know that those moments of faith and prayer built up my faithfulness as I matured.

Because of those small displays of faith, I was later able to conquer many obstacles through having faith in God and His promises for me.

Through my own experiences, I have experienced different measures of faith. Some I'm not proud of and others I am una-shamed to announce to everyone. But as is written in Romans 12:3, *"Instead, think sensibly, as God has distributed a measure of faith to each one."* I believe that we all experience faith with differ-ent measures. I feel blessed to know this gift of faith. This is one of the gifts God has given each one of us, and I believe it is ours to discover and use.

As I continued to research, I came across another verse, this time in Matthew 17:20: *"For truly I tell you, if you have faith the size of a mustard seed, you will tell this mountain, 'Move from here to there,' and it will move. Nothing will be impossible for you."*

When I take a deeper look at this verse, I compare it to agriculture and nature. It reminds me that if I plant a seed, in order for it to grow into its true being it needs to be watered and nurtured each day. The same is true of our faith. I need to use it daily by trusting God with small things, and also big things, and by doing so I strengthen and increase my faith.

I didn't always understand faith and I was sometimes impatient, to say the least. I felt that I just didn't have the kind faith that's written about in Matthew 17:20. I tend to want to control my situation, and if I can't I can end up frustrated and faithless.

Then, one day, I had to put the true meaning of faith into action.

It's hard for me to describe the events that took place that cold Saturday morning in January without remembering the trauma that still sometimes haunts me. My husband had a business trip and he'd left early. My children and I often hung out with family to make the days shorter, and to distract us from missing him on his travel days.

That day, we decided to visit my sister and spend the day at her home so the cousins could play together. As I sipped tea at the dining room table with my sister, the children played in a nearby room. My sister and I sat together sharing stories, peacefully enjoying the afternoon…

And that's when I heard it, the screaming and screeching. These noises were coming from my son!

What I saw next shocked me. While playing around and jumping on the bed, he had fallen and landed on a metal dumbbell that had been carelessly left on the bed. He now had a deep wound to his forehead, so deep that I literally saw the bone of his skull.

I froze in terror and shock. I kept reminding myself to stay calm because if everyone saw me panic we would lose control.

A voice kept whispering in my ear: *"I got this."* I thought it was my own voice at first, until I realized that it was God. He was in control and I had to turn the situation over to Him.

Lead the way, I silently told Him.

And so I grabbed my son's sweatshirt, which was laid beside my chair, and pressed it up against the wound to stop the bleeding. I quickly called 911.

The story gets even more interesting because this day, being mid-January, was cold and snowy. The emergency vehicles would take longer than expected due to delays on the road.

It took several persistent phone calls to emergency and a very long hour before the ambulance showed up. This left me frustrated and annoyed, and I thought about driving us to the hospital myself. But I knew the roads weren't safe and things could get worse that way.

When the ambulance finally arrived, it took us to the community hospital. This wasn't my first choice, since I would have preferred he be taken to the children's hospital. However, the weather was terrible and the community hospital had been within five kilometres. Besides, the EMT made the choice. I had to remain in faith, knowing and trusting that God was in control.

I prayed silently and in full authority and faith. I know God was listening and was holding me up the whole time.

When we got to the hospital, we were immediately met by the triage nurse. We were then taken to the emergency room where my son was taken care of. A few hours and a few stitches later, I am grateful that he turned out to be completely okay. There was no long-term damage, only a superficial scar.

When I look back, I thank God that my faith was bigger than my fear, and that by remaining calm my son also remained calm. I remember his deep stare as he looked up at me for answers and assurance that everything would be okay. I remained calm and faithful, believing that God knew how to handle this and that he would be all right.

Whenever I exercise faith instead of fear, fear has no power over me. It has no power over my mind.

When I choose to turn my fear into faith, I notice that faith can transform life-altering situations and decisions.

With every experience I go through, there is a lesson, and with every lesson I get stronger. I choose to give God control because I know that He understands it all and knows exactly what He's doing.

While at church one Sunday morning, the pastor said, "The gift of faith is that it sees the challenge and runs straight into it. It doesn't say, 'How do I get out of this?' It says, 'How do I get through this?'" This message has stayed with me. I now welcome any situation that comes my way because I know God is with me. I have faith in all His ways.

Nine

BALANCE

IN MY LATE THIRTIES, I LEARNED THE TRUE MEANING OF BALANCE. During my *in between* journey, I started attending another type of therapy session, called kinesiology. Kinesiology is the scientific study of human body movement. It is the use of muscle testing to identify imbalances in the body's structural, chemical, and emotional energy. It can improve the performance of the human body while it's at work or in our daily activities.

This type of therapy was part of my recovery program. I didn't want to go, but I committed to it and attended the four-week program three times per week for one-hour sessions. Since it is known that exercise improves mental health and can reduce anxiety and depression, improving a negative mood and mindset, it was important to participate in these exercise sessions.

In these sessions, I exercised and got my body back in physical motion, pushing myself to exercise and move even when I really didn't want to. I had no motivation and was so tired from mental exhaustion.

One session, I mistakenly brought my daughter's shoes instead of my own and I had to do the whole session with only my socks on. I hadn't been motived to begin with; imagine how I felt now that I was shoeless. I was embarrassed and my level of enthusiasm went from zero to negative zero, if that's even possible.

At my first session, we started with a quick physical evaluation, completing several health forms, and going through a question-and-answer period which would allow my coach to plan out a program designed specifically for me.

At the second session, my coach laid out the program he had designed. I accepted it, feeling a little sceptical at first. Instead of being negative, I accepted the plan and went along with it. Believe me, it felt like nothing more than a waste of time since I could do all this same stuff on my own or at the local gym.

On the first real workout day, my coach demonstrated each workout I had to do. It seemed easy enough—some treadmill walking, some weights for my arms, pushups, planks… it was the same basic exercise routine I had already done before.

But then he showed me the wooden balance board and told me to balance myself on it for thirty seconds for three repetitions. I had no idea why I had to do this. In all honesty, I thought it was ridiculous. I sometimes wanted to skip that exercise or just pretend I'd done it. But conviction would set in and I'd do it regardless.

That was one of the hardest exercises, but I later realized it was also one of the most important.

About two weeks after my sessions finished, the reason for using that balance board hit me. Balancing on that wooden plank made me realize how important balance is, not only physical balance but in other ways: emotional balance, sleep balance, nutritional balance, career balance, and spiritual balance.

I learned that

emotional balance is the ability of the mind and body to maintain equilibrium and flexibility in moments of challenge and change. Having balance in our emotions promotes physical health and wellbeing.

However, being out of balance emotionally, and avoiding emotional stress, often causes a person to suppress feelings which can lead to anxiety and even depression. By setting proper boundaries and limits, one can maintain a healthy emotional balance.

Another area where balance is important is sleep. A sleep-deprived person is most often irritated, frustrated, and uncomfortable, because a lack of rest leads to unbalanced sleep. We are designed for rest in order to recharge and start each day fresh. A good night's sleep can reduce stress, improve your memory, lower your blood pressure, and set you in a better mood, just to name a few of its benefits. A bad sleep can affect your mental health and lead to high blood pressure, diabetes, heart problems, obesity, and depression. Chronic sleep deprivation even affects your appearance. Most adults need seven hours of sleep each night, and maintaining a regular bedtime and routine can help in the development of a healthy and balanced sleep cycle.

My career is another area where I've learned to practice a healthy balance. I've encountered many people who are unbalanced in this way. People are wired from a very young age to work as hard as they can in order to have the life they've dreamed of.

Not everyone has the opportunity to work for themselves, being able to create their own schedule, so how does one maintain a healthy work-life balance? How can they not take their stress from the office home to their loved ones?

The answer can be found in setting a boundary at work. Setting yourself up with unrealistic goals can create stress, which leads to taking that stress back with you to your home and family. Children don't need to be affected by their parents' unhealthy stress.

I'm not saying that children need to see a completely stress-free life. Absolutely not. That would be unrealistic and would mean setting them up for a fairy tale life that doesn't exist. What I mean is that we need to demonstrate to our children how to set and stick to healthy limits.

Exercise is another area where balance is needed. Setting realistic exercise routines, and seeing them through consistently, leads to good health. You don't need to constantly try different exercise programs just because you're not getting the results you want. When you choose to be balanced and consistent with your exercise, you will most likely notice good results over time as opposed to having unrealistic exercise goals.

It's also important to have balance in the area of food and nutrition. If you choose to eat or drink more of one item than another, your body will react in a certain manner and give you a warning single that something else is lacking.

For example, on days when I choose to drink excessive amounts of coffee and not enough water, my body signals me with a headache. It never fails. The result is instantaneous for me. Being consistent and balanced with our nutrition is highly important.

Food is fuel, and without it we cannot go on. The vitamins and nutrients we receive from food must be balanced so that each and every part of our body gets exactly what it needs in order to remain healthy.

I'm not a certified nutritionist, but I've been blessed to have found a network of very intelligent nutritionists I rely on so I can be well informed about what my body lacks. I recognized that my nutrition was unbalanced and so I chose to improve what goes into my body. It has changed the way I feel, physically and mentally.

Balance is key to everything I do. Once I started to implement a healthy and balanced life, my frustrations began to ease. The stuff that used to irritate me no longer bothered me. Life started to feel more comfortable.

In conclusion, I've also noticed that having a balanced spiritual and prayer relationship with God has led me to go through life with love and knowledge. When I lack in any area spiritually, I start to lose certainty and fears slip in. That's when I know that I'm out of balance.

Whenever my mornings are rushed and I don't take time for prayer, devotion, and reading, I end up in messes that I have a very hard time cleaning up. And in times when I've felt that my life is out of balance, I can simply pray for the Lord's help to remain focused on the things that are most important, preventing distractions from stealing my time and attention from God.

Ten

FORGIVENESS

MY MOTHER IS THE LOVE PILLAR OF OUR FAMILY. A HUMBLE WOMAN with a forgiving heart, she loves and fears the Lord and lives to serve God and her family. She is the type who keeps her emotions to herself. Growing up, I remember that she very rarely showed any anger, regret, or remorse.

As I look back on my childhood, I have learned much about my mother. She rose early in the morning to ensure she spent alone time with God first. She also made sure breakfast, lunch, and dinner was always served to us. She loved and served the Lord with all her heart and soul.

Her Bible followed her from the kitchen table to the living room couch, and wherever else she went. She prayed till heaven roared and then prayed some more.

She has a gentle tone and grace about her. She practices patience like no other. Frustration was a foreign word to me, as were words like *hate* and *revenge.*

I think back at how she was always able to remain calm during stormy situations.

My mother taught me the importance of peace and patience. When I find myself in situations where I'm about to blast off, so to speak, her gentle tone whispers in my ear and I can remind myself that I have the ability to stay calm.

During my *in between* journey, I've learned the true meaning of forgiveness and moving on. The Bible also indicates the importance of forgiveness. Colossians 3:13 says that *"bearing with one another and forgiving one another if anyone has a grievance against another. Just as the Lord has forgiven you, so you are also to forgive."*

As hard as it is at times, we should extend grace to others, just as we have been showed grace from Jesus Christ.

I have learned that when I forgive others, I'm not telling them that what they've done is okay. Instead I am releasing them to God, letting go of the hold they have over me.

As Ephesians 4:31–32 tells us, *"Get rid of all bitterness, rage and anger, brawling and slander, along with every form of malice. Be kind and compassionate to one another, forgiving each other, just as in Christ God forgave you"* (NIV).

God is telling us to get rid of all—not some, but all—bitterness, rage, and anger. He goes on to tell us to get rid of brawling (in other words, fighting) and slander (telling false statements to damage a person's reputation). The verse goes on to say we must eliminate every desire to do evil.

How can we practice this in our daily lives? God further tells to be kind and compassionate to one another. Being kind is a quality that shows others friendliness, generosity, and care. Compassion is about demonstrating understanding and concern. And lastly, God tells to forgive—to truly forgive, which means to stop feeling angry or resentful towards those who have hurt us, whether intentionally or unintentionally.

As a mom to two children of middle school age, it has been revealed to me that we do what we have to do to get through the tough days, the sad days, and the hard days. Sometimes we function and other times we only pretend, so to speak, to make it through.

I know now what I didn't know when I was younger: motherhood is a job, a job that requires so much. Oftentimes it's a job that no one acknowledges, not even the people who are closest to you, which are your children and spouse. And when a person's work isn't acknowledged or valued, the result can be a lack of motivation, burnout, anxiety, and even depression.

Yes, motherhood is work. At times it has come naturally and easily to me, and at other times I'm merely surviving. When I can't figure out an answer to a problem in my parenting journey, I turn to others for help. Even though their advice might be wrong, I'm still willing to try anything to get through the worst struggles.

Only now do I understand that my mother did all she knew to do—and that was to love us, shelter us, influence us, clothe us, and feed us.

I remember always having good food. Most of my friends would beg to come over after school and on weekends just to have a taste of her spaghetti sauce. She prepared food with delicious Italian flavours that left almost everyone wanting more.

I also remember her rising early every day to set herself through prayer, worship music, devotion, and coffee. As a young teenager, I just wanted to yell out, "Lower the volume! I'm trying to sleep!" But now, in my *in between* motherhood, I actually thank her for her example. She has shown me how to remain strong and capable throughout the day. It isn't always easy to rise early, and some weekends I do indulge in some sleeping in. But for my consistent morning routine, I am grateful to my mother.

In this stage of my life, I have had several opportunities to forgive. I forgave myself for my feelings of frustration towards others. I felt guilty for these emotions, but I found freedom in forgiving myself for them. This has helped me move forward when I've been stuck.

Each moment of forgiveness has opened me and healed me. I noticed that there were many things in my life that I wasn't letting go of. I had held on to what I thought other people thought of me, allowing others to control parts of my mind, just by thinking about what they expected and thought of me.

In a moment of prayer one day, I realized that I had to release all this. When I thought about their expectations of me, my relationships with them were toxic and unhealthy. As soon as I released them, I began to take the good from that person. Only then did true forgiveness take place. I'm happy to say that I have healed many relationships during my *in between* journey simply by choosing forgiveness.

In a private moment in prayer with God one day, I asked Him to show me my broken relationships and heal them. I asked Him to restore truth. I realized that I had been holding onto another very toxic belief—that whenever I did something that wasn't aligned with God's will, I couldn't ask for His forgiveness. Instead I held onto the guilt, which kept me from being free. Even though I was forgiven, I was still allowing the guilt to control me.

Then I remembered that once God forgives my sin, He also removes guilt. Once I believed His truth and His promise, I was able to live a forgiven and guilt-free life.

Another day I prayed, "Lord, by Your grace I am forgiven of my past, as well as the guilt that wants to linger, so why is this guilt still lingering? I will not allow my past failures to spoil the future You have for me."

Once I believed the words, I started living out my future. I knew that I was forgiven, and God's Word confirmed it for me in Hebrews 10:17–18: *"I will never again remember their sins and their lawless acts. Now where there is forgiveness of these, there is no longer an offering for sin."*

Eleven

LOVE

I HAVE BEEN BLESSED WITH FAMILY, AND IN THIS CHAPTER I WILL speak of some very special women in my life, including my mother and the two sisters she gifted me with. These women have been, and still are, the foundation of who I am. I will try my best to articulate the way they love and unconditionally care about me.

The love they display can only come from a place that is given to us by God. They are unselfish and caring on so many levels. But most of all they have been a true support throughout my *in between* stage.

Although they both mean the same to me and I love them equally, they are also distinct in their love for me. They show their love in different ways. They have both been a big influence on my life.

One of my sisters has a heart of compassion like no other. Her tender voice and gentle words are healing. In times of lowliness and despair, I turn to her. Her accepting character is enough to allow me to pour out whatever emotion I've bottled up.

She has taught me very important life lessons, and when it comes to love she has taught me that love heals all. Love secures. She has portrayed love throughout her life, and by that she's taught me that we were designed by God to help others, to be kind, and to not judge.

She has demonstrated that it's possible to give of yourself, volunteer, and learn new things. She has also taught me to never stop learning, never stop asking, and never stop persevering. Her devotion has taught me to never give up.

She has also most definitely taught me that love is free. No one should have to pay for love, and most certainly no one should be guilted into love. God's love is free and given to each of us freely.

I've been blessed to witness her relationship with God, and I've been blessed to learn from her.

My other sister is a true example of perseverance and faith. Her love for me has always been shown through encouragement and motivation. She believes in me in more ways than I can believe in myself sometimes.

Her love and devotion to God and her family has helped shape me to be the mother and wife I am today. She puts God first in everything she does, and this can be seen throughout her life.

She is strong and courageous. She sets her mind and ways on those things that are good and she gets them done, no matter the obstacles or timeline. She perseveres and persists in ways I haven't seen in anyone else.

Her love for her family is consistent and clear. She's always praying, always believing, always declaring the goodness of God on their lives, and always trusting God to deliver on His promises.

There were so many times when I didn't believe in myself, especially throughout my *in between* journey. Honestly, if it wasn't for my sisters and their support, love, and confidence in me, I don't think I would have been able to take that leap of faith and believe in myself to take on a new challenge and career. They have shown me what it truly means to take a leap of faith.

What I admire most about these two women is that we are different in many ways, yet we gather and agree on the most important values, and for that we have the number one woman to thank: our mother. She carried us, cried for us, raised us, prayed for us, and interceded for us.

There is another kind of love I share with another human being, and that is the man God created to spend his adult life with me: my husband. I know

---

many people refer to their spouse as their better half, but in my case he's more than just my better half; he's the piece God created to fit my puzzle.

This man has given me the true experience of unconditional love.

Although love is free, marriage is also devotion and work, something you accomplish together as a couple. I realize that I cannot expect to plant a garden and have it grow on its own. I have to tend, prune, and nurture it in order to get the bountiful produce. The same is true in marriage. I've been married for quite some time, I knew my husband before that for many years, and I can assure you that every single day this man is prayed for.

Throughout our marriage, we've experienced some downs. Some we fought through together, and others we fought on our own. When I say we fought on our own, I don't mean that the other didn't fight; I mean that the fight for the other was silent. I don't always show my true feelings, even to my husband. Maybe it's because of shame, or maybe pride, but sometimes I would prefer to battle silently.

I have come to the conclusion, though, that love is the answer to all my battles. Once I offer love and invite love into my situation, then and only then does healing take place. Only then am I open to solutions, open to the possibility that healing can happen.

I have also experienced another kind of love, the one mentioned in Mark 12:31: *"Love your neighbor as yourself. There is no other command greater than these."*

Only love makes us do the unimaginable for another, and for me that was to step in and help save another's life. I had a moment in my life when God chose me to be an anchor and lifeline to two small children involved in a drowning accident that nearly caused all three of us to suffer an unimaginable death.

I remember that day vividly. It occurred on a family summer trip that could have turned into a nightmare. Instead it was filled with miracles, praise, and meekness.

On the second day of our summer getaway, we headed towards the beach. It was a hot, humid afternoon and the children were especially excited about going into the water. However, upon our arrival at the parking station, our excitement was crushed when we were turned away due to the beach being too full.

Highly disappointed, we decided to still make the best of this gorgeous summer day.

The friends we were with led us to a more remote area that had a lake and small shore. This particular area wasn't under city surveillance, so we could swim at our own risk. We chose to stay very close together and make sure the children didn't venture away from the shore. We knew that lakes can be unpredictable with their currents and depth. It wouldn't be worth risking our lives by swimming too far out.

We sat close to the water in beach chairs and set up the coolers we had brought along so we could enjoy an afternoon picnic. Before long we all entered the lake and stood in a circle, refreshed from the summer heat.

The rustic scenery and beauty of nature was outstanding. We were surrounded by trees, rocks, and even some rapids. We listened to the sound of flowing water, children playing, splashing water, families laughing, and birds chirping. It was a splendid day.

Suddenly, my attention was drawn to two small children who had been left alone in the water, unsupervised. There was no guardian in sight, and they seemed to be about two years old and nine years old. They were about twelve feet away, and at first they just seemed to be making playful motions. Then the younger child grappled onto the older one, trying to scream for help as they were both being pushed down into the water.

I reacted quicker than at any other time in my life and started swimming towards them. I'm not a professional swimmer. I occasionally swim and know the basics, but I had no idea how to rescue drowning children… and no idea what would happen once I reached them. But I sensed an urging to help these children, who I felt would die if someone didn't get to them quickly.

Once I reached the children, their flailing arms pulled me into the water. I swallowed so much water and had no time to think, as they kept pulling me down. I wrapped my arms around them, I tried hard to swim closer to shore so I would be close enough for the others to help; it was too dangerous for them to come out to us. The water was deep, cold, and I couldn't reach the bottom.

Each time my head miraculously made its way up out of the water, I drew a breath and yelled for help. While under I cried out to God in silence. Each time I came up, my vision blurred and the sound was muffled.

I pleaded for a miracle, for someone to pull us closer to shore. I remember thinking I had no more strength, that it was time to let go and give up. But then I reminded myself that giving up was *not* an option. I had a life ahead of me. This was not the way I was going down.

I didn't have any flashes of my life, as some have said about near-death experiences. Instead my future flashed in front of me, and a hope that this was a simple rescue mission God needed me to attend to.

I remember hearing the muffled screams of my husband, my daughter, and our friends. I locked my eyes on them for a moment, and through my blurred vision I saw the fright in their eyes. With every breath I had left, I shouted out to God, "Help me!"

And in that moment, a miracle happened. It felt as though someone was pushing me up from under the water. I had no more energy, but time seemingly stood still. In the natural, I kept swimming as best I could, bringing these two children and I closer to shore.

All of a sudden, a bystander reached out his arm and in that moment his arm seemed to me like a long six-foot branch. I reached out for it and was brought to safety.

The children were taken by others nearby and they eventually reunited with their father.

As we sat there afterward, shocked yet grateful, my daughter told me that the first thing she had wanted to do was swim out to me—but she had known that was impossible, so instead she had prayed and never stopped praying. She'd cried out to God with certainty that I would make it out alive. She told me how scared she had been, but she'd also felt confident knowing that God answers our prayers.

My friend later told me that she had been agreeing with my daughter's prayer and praying right alongside her.

I had obeyed God's instruction to love your neighbour as yourself. I was obedient, and in return the lives of those children were spared.

We all learned several lessons that day. For me, I learned the meaning of the term "divine appointment." That afternoon, I was at the appointed time and place. I also learned something about God's protection, and about praying in the name of Jesus and the true meaning of being in agreement with one's fellow Christians.

Whatever happened that day, I know that it happened for the greater good, as indicated in Romans 8:28: *"We know that all things work together for the good of those who love God, who are called according to his purpose."*

Once again, love is the answer and God works for the good of those who love Him.

Twelve

FEAR

I DESCRIBE THE SOUND OF FEAR AS THE VOICE WE HAVE DEVELOPED in our brain. Maybe it's our own voice, or the voice of our parents, a sibling, or a friend. Whoever's voice it is, it's the voice we hear when we are afraid.

I now remind myself that this voice isn't real.

I once heard that fear can be thought of as an acronym for "false evidence appearing real." When I take the time to consider this, it makes so much sense. Fear isn't an actual object; it isn't real. It is a belief that my mind accepts.

Fears shows up in different forms. It may manifest as a fear of public speaking, or a fear of driving, or a fear of doctor appointments. Whatever it is, we become scared when we don't know the outcome of a certain situation.

As a child, there were many moments when fear attacked me. When I was six, I went to the mall one day with my mother and siblings. I don't remember the moment I lost sight of my mom, but I do remember the moment I realized she was no longer there.

As a mom today, I try my best to hold on tight to my active children. However, we all know that sometimes outings can be eventful and we lose track.

The memory is vivid. I can feel the fear rising up in my chest, my throat tightening, and my palms sweating. The fear made my mind race. My eyes searched frantically. I felt so scared and alone.

Now, all those emotions were real. I'm not saying you should ignore your feelings. Instead what I'm trying to say is that the scenarios I made up in my mind that day weren't real. The only thing that was real was the situation—I was in the mall without my mother. But I wasn't alone. Not only was the mall filled with other shoppers and sales attendants, I was also with one of my siblings.

Had I been equipped with the proper tools to deal with that situation, I could have stopped myself from thinking up the worst-case scenarios. I would have known that fear is nothing but a liar.

As a mother, I try to provide my children with the tools they need in order to face their fears. They will be put in situations and scenarios that are out of our control. If I teach them how to author their own thoughts properly, if I teach them that they have authority over their own fears, if I teach them that their mindset is their most important tool, I will have given them the solution to overcome their fear.

It is my responsibility as my children's mother to instill in them these tools.

When our children suffer attacks of fear and anxiety, it becomes a very serious issue. The world they once knew as innocent, loving, and fun gives way to toxic environments, some which are out of our control. Perhaps schoolmates use words they've never heard before, leaving them to figure out what's going on.

During my *in between* journey, I learned the importance of communicating daily with my children. This is one of the ways I help them develop the skills and support they need. It requires a lot of work, because the way we communicate with a ten-year-old is definitely not the same way we communicate with our peers.

In order for our children to fully express their feelings, they need to know that we understand them, that we aren't judging them, and that most of all they won't be punished for what they tell us.

Children want to feel safe and loved. They want to know that no matter what they tell us, our view of them won't change.

If you're able to establish trust between yourself and your child, you will give them the tools to face fear.

We can't eliminate or control what gets thrown at our children, but we can teach them how to deal with fear. I showed my child that prayer, along with breathing tools, makes a big difference when faced with a fearful situation.

When I'm with my children, I want them to be able to hear my voice guiding them, knowing that through prayer and calling out to God, fear-stricken situations can turn into peaceful ones. Instead of being stuck with fear, they can direct their minds from fear to faith.

I recently got to experience this firsthand. With only one day's notice, I was asked to do a reading at a family wedding. Of course I gladly accepted the opportunity. It was an honour, actually, as I was going to share this occasion with my daughter, who was also doing a reading. Doing this together would give me a chance to show her that fear is a battle we can overcome and win.

What's interesting is that my biggest fear used to be public speaking. Days prior to any public speaking event, I would develop a crippling anxiety that wouldn't allow me to sleep. I would stop eating and my throat would lock up.

But this time something was different. This time, my mindset was renewed. I not only told myself that I could do this, but I pictured myself up there. I pushed away all anxiety. I protected my thoughts from the fear that came my way, which was nothing but lies trying to make their way in. This time, I told myself, I could do this. I didn't allow fear to set in.

As I stood up there, getting ready to speak, I stopped for a few seconds and stared into the audience.

"Don't rush," I told myself. "Take your time, make sure to be heard, adjust yourself, and be comfortable."

I threw fear right out that church door and embraced the woman I was. I allowed others to see me as a strong, confident, godly woman as I delivered a passage of scripture with all my heart.

That day, I was proud of myself. Most importantly, I was proud to have shown my daughter how to beat fear.

Growing up, I often heard at church that there are 365 "fear not" references in the Bible. God has given us the authority to fear not. He knows that the enemy wants to attack our minds with fear and lies, as that's the enemy's way to decrease our faith and hope. That's why He has provided hundreds of messages telling us not to fear.

Isaiah 41:10 tells us, *"Fear not, for I am with you; be not dismayed, for I am your God. I will strengthen you, yes, I will help you, I will uphold you with My righteous right hand"* (NKJV).

This is God's promise. We can choose to accept it, or we can choose to reject it. Accepting His promise leads to a life of fulfillment, love, faith, and hope.

Choosing to fear not doesn't mean we ignore our fear. Just the opposite. It means that we face our fear. I choose to be honest with myself and bring my fear to light, and by doing this I break the chain that has been created. God knows my struggle with fear, and that's why I believe He gave us 365 reminders not to fear.

Once I began to understand that fear is a spiritual battle, I was able to conquer it. Fear is part of the enemy's schemes, and by holding me in fear he was trying to keep me quiet and unsuccessful.

In Ephesians 6:10–18, the apostle Paul tells us to put on the full armour of God. This isn't the physical armour of God; it speaks of a supernatural type of armour.

Finally, be strengthened by the Lord and by his vast strength. Put on the full armor of God so that you can stand against the schemes of the devil. For our struggle is not against flesh and blood, but against the rulers, against the authorities, against the cosmic powers of this darkness, against evil, spiritual forces in the heavens. For this reason take up the full armor of God, so that you may be able to resist in the evil day, and having prepared everything, to take your stand. Stand, therefore, with truth like a belt around your waist, righteousness like armor on your chest, and your feet sandaled with readiness for the gospel of peace. In every situation take up the shield of faith with which you can extinguish all the flaming arrows of the evil one. Take the helmet of salvation and the sword of the Spirit—which is the word of God. Pray at all times in the Spirit with every prayer and request, and stay alert with all perseverance and intercession for all the saints. (Ephesians 6:10–18)

I decided in my *in between* journey to finally use the armour as it is meant to be used. I learned that God gave His children spiritual weapons. Some of us aren't yet aware we have these weapons.

Today, I hope you will see the passage with the enlightened eyes of your heart.

As I continued to study this passage, I noticed that I can cast out fear. The enemy tries to cause fights in our own families, dividing homes. And as long as fear is at the centre of a family, divisions remain.

1. The first piece of armour is truth. Ephesians 6:14 tells us, *"Stand, therefore, with truth like a belt around your waist…"*

As a believer, my truth is the Bible, which is God's Word. It is the foundation upon which I stand. Once I learned how to consistently stand firm in the truth, I was able to conquer my battles. I learned to keep truth close to me. I let truth surround me like a belt so I can be equipped for any spiritual battles that come my way. Once I knew my truth, and that I wasn't willing to compromise my truth, I was able to stand firm.

2. The second piece of armour is righteousness. Ephesians 6:14 adds, *"…righteousness like armor on your chest."*

To be righteous is to be free from guilt or sin. When I wear righteousness on my chest, which in turn means that it's in my heart, I use it as a shield from temptations so that I can rely on the love of God. When I'm struggling with certain areas in my life that I know aren't right, I choose to do right and remind myself of God's righteousness.

3. The third piece of armour is peace. Ephesians 6:15 says, *"…and your feet sandaled with readiness for the gospel of peace."* This verse tells me to stand firm on my feet and walk in peace in everything I do.

Almost every day I am challenged to stay peaceful and calm. Conversations with others can easily turn into strong disagreements, stealing my peace from me. I need to remind myself that I am in control of my peace. I am the one who allows peace to enter or escape my mind.

By starting each day firm on my feet and in peace, I am made ready to conquer what the world throws at me.

4. The fourth piece of armour is faith. Ephesians 6:16 says, *"In every situation take up the shield of faith with which you can extinguish all the flaming arrows of the enemy."* Wearing faith as a shield reminds me that whenever unbelief comes my way, I am to put up my shield and protect my beliefs and faith.

We live in a world where opinions are perceived as truth, and truth is perceived as being insane. Being rooted in the truth of God's Word is a very specific and important way of wearing our shield. Most people I come across are quick to react to others' comments. However, most people react without ever taking the proper time to study what the truth really is. They remain convinced that they're right just because they've formed their own opinion of what it should be.

5. The fifth piece of armour is salvation. Ephesians 6:17 tells us, *"Take the helmet of salvation…"*

This verse reminds me that once I accept the salvation of Jesus, the Holy Spirit lives in me, protecting me with a helmet over my brain. Whenever false opinions are directed my way, I know how to answer in truth. Starting my day with devotion and prayer are ways in which I choose to wear my helmet of salvation.

6. The sixth piece of armour is the Holy Spirit. Ephesians 6:17 adds, *"…and the sword of the Spirit—which is the word of God."*

Once I experienced the Holy Spirit as my helper, I became fearless, as though I was holding a sword of protection. I recognized that the Holy Spirit had been sent to me as a help—and I must not be afraid to accept that help.

For me, the Word of God symbolizes the sword. With God's Word I am able to defeat all my enemies.

Knowing and continuing to study God's Word has helped me greatly. Whenever I'm being attacked, whether the attack comes from another person or from emotions like sadness, anxiety, or depression, I remind myself of what God has promised me. This makes me ready for battle with my biblical sword, which is His Word. It's just like holding a real sword before battle.

7. The seventh piece of armour is prayer. Ephesians 6:18 tells us, *"Pray at all times in the Spirit with every prayer and request, and stay alert with all perseverance and intercession for all the saints."*

I start each day with prayer. When I pray, I allow myself to be in the presence of God. I allow myself to be surrounded by love and not be judged. When I do so, something amazing happens; I experience peace, love, and protection. I choose to pray continually throughout the day. And I choose to pray before bed too.

The enemy wants to keep us surrounded by fear so that we don't succeed, because success equals positivity, love, thankfulness, passion, and all other good things. Fear is a liar and the enemy tries to feed people with lies to keep us in a state of fear.

Whenever I was paralyzed by fear, my throat would lock, making it very difficult to breathe. I used to ignore this, hoping it would go away on its own. But I have learned that listening to my body and acknowledging what's happening is a good start to overcoming fear.

I quietly took the time to speak to my body and ask myself, what is truly going on? I started by speaking to God in prayer. I asked for things to be revealed to me, for comfort, for a sound mind, and for peace to return to me as I make the decision not to let fear in anymore.

This has helped most when I look back at how much good has come from past fearful situations. I also remind myself with songs, books, and verses that God is good and that the future will be okay when I make different choices—because I no longer live in the past or in fear, and I refuse to listen to lies.

Thirteen
PERSEVERANCE

THE MORNING I SENT OUT THE RESIGNATION LETTER, IT WAS A Monday. The letter explained to my employer why I had chosen not to return to work. I also summed up the months of counselling I had gone through and my reasons for choosing not to remain stuck.

It felt good. Scary, but good. Fear-stricken, but still good.

As I typed it up, I reminded myself to keep using every tool I had acquired throughout my *in between* journey. If I didn't remind myself, the vicious cycle would just come back and make me stuck once more.

Sitting at my kitchen table in silence, all alone, I felt like I was about to become crippled by fear. I started to feel my throat tighten, my tongue glued to my pallet, my bones starting to shut down. I couldn't move from my chair or speak aloud. As I felt heaviness settle over me, I wanted to call Ruth for support and guidance.

But this time, it didn't get me. This time, I chose to change my mindset and focus on my purpose. This time, I *spoke*. This time,

I *moved*. This time, I *worshipped*. I fought. I surrendered. I was surrounded by God, surrounded by His amazing love, by faith, by truth, by words of encouragement. I was surrounded by belief.

I have been given a spirit of courage and wisdom, and this time I used it. I realized that all the lies flying in my direction were exactly that… lies. I chose not to believe them. And I chose not to create any erroneous ideas of what others were thinking.

Soon it was done—the email was sent and over with.

Actually, that wasn't difficult at all. It's amazing. Once I truly let go of something, it seems easy and painless. To let go of something means to release it. To loosen one's hold.

And so this is where my beginning began. I let go of the chains that had held me down, allowing myself to take a step forward into my purpose.

I now realize that

-----

my life is a gift. In this life, I get to choose and speak and be heard. I no longer live under bondage and fear.

I've not only found a great mentor on this journey, but great leaders. The difference between a boss and a leader is that a boss manages while a leader inspires. A leader is helpful, inspirational, and allows others to think creatively and be themselves. In my experience, I've noticed that most people are looking for leaders… not bosses.

One morning while praying, I asked God to give me *my* word. I prayed, "Lord, give me one word to describe me, one word that I can use every day of my life to better myself and fulfill my purpose."

I didn't expect a vocal response, but what I got surprised me.

In that moment, a memory trickled back to me of a time when I was sitting at my desk at my old job. There had been several frames in that office, each featuring a word, and one of them had somehow ended up on my desk.

The word was *perseverance.*

What is perseverance? Perseverance is doing something despite difficulties and delays. It is persistence, determination, and purposefulness.

All those years, I looked at that word every day—and years later, I finally did persevere. I had worked with all my heart and dedicated all my strength and power to this job that I came to every day. But along the way, I had missed something. I had lacked success.

Success is the outcome of perseverance. It took me many years and one burnout to realize that I hadn't climbed up the ladder of success at that job. I was stagnant. Even worse, my value weakened a bit more every day.

I came to realize that my only way to achieve success was to move out of this career. I had absolutely no opportunity for growth there. Even worse, I had allowed myself to work harder and harder, actually thinking that victory would happen.

My main focus today is not the past but the way in which God made the word *perseverance* visible to me several years ago and allowed it to take on new significance. I've finally developed the courage to practice it.

This part of my journey is actually the best part. I get to say no to fear and goodbye to manipulation. I now persevere to gain success.

And so my journey to finding my purpose begins here. I'm headed in the right direction as long as I stay focused and grounded in the truth every day.

Proverbs 31:15 tells us, *"She rises while it is still night and provides food for her household and portions for her female servants."* This simply means that the woman spoken of in this verse doesn't indulge in too much sleep, but rises early to get the best results by simply dedicating her day to God and planning her day for the household. When a person rises early, they get a head start and set the tone for their day.

In my journey, my early rising consists of alone time with God alongside my husband. We make it a priority to just sit and enjoy each other's company in the early morning. In these moments, we share special prayers, readings, devotions, and conversations. We also share our dreams and fears. We listen to each other, encourage each other, and edify each other.

Morning is the most important part of my day, and my favourite part. In the morning, right before the kids wake up, I can hear the singing of the birds. I love the part of the day when it's still dark out, but suddenly the sky brightens with daylight. That part is so special. During these times, I get to meditate on God's Word and learn about His lovingkindness. I get to feel His presence. I get to be still and just be.

Of course, there are still some setbacks. Some mornings I'm a little more tired than usual and my motivation is lacking. On these mornings, I must work the hardest to adjust my attitude. On these mornings, I'm a little frustrated and sometimes sad.

There's no particular reason why the sadness appears, but I've experienced enough in my life to know that it's because something in my life is out of balance. On these particular mornings, it's important for me to sit back and review the past few days and weeks. When I take the time and look back and dig deep, I'll notice that there's a common pattern, something I haven't dealt with, something I've ignored.

I've learned to journal about my emotions and dreams. By doing so, I usually find solutions to the problems in my life. I just don't want to accept the answer sometimes, because the answer requires me to make some adjustments, whether it be in my attitude, my mindset, or something in my routine.

I'm happy to say that I have now crossed over from my *in between* stage to living my purpose. As I crossed over, my days have felt brighter, full of hope and love. I no longer have sleepless nights. Waking up in the morning, I am fully rested, and my mind is alert and focused. Thoughts of fear and dread no longer cripple me. I have started a new career. I take on projects that I love and I look forward to what the future holds.

I now focus on enjoying a life filled with knowledge and faith. I renew my mind daily and focus on all of God's promises. I focus on helping others. I also take time each day to be thankful for allowing myself to be brave enough and strong enough to overcome my *in between*.

When I look back, I remember days when I couldn't even imagine having a new beginning, but here I am and here I go. My next chapter awaits. I continue to meet new people along the way, each one telling me of their struggles. I'm grateful that I get to offer them a listening ear and compassionate heart. I'm also grateful that God chose me and has pointed them in my direction. I get to pray for each one of them.

Finally, I'm grateful that I get to plant a seed of hope that years later will flourish into a beautiful harvest. Several people have called me years after an encounter with me to let me know how God has impacted and changed their lives. Just one word changed how they think and how they want to live their lives.

That's the seed I'm referring to. All it takes is a listening ear, a compassionate heart, and His Word.

People often say, "I'm just surviving, just making it through each day." It saddens me to know that so many people are suffering and battling on their own. They hide their stories and don't talk about them, but I realize that everyone has their own story to tell.

Someone, somewhere is in the middle of a silent fight today. I pray and hope that this book will be a helpful guide and an opening for others who want to know more about God and discover who He is and why He created us. I hope people can do their own search and gain answers to learn more about what their purpose is.

Remember: this is not the end. It's just the beginning.

www.ingramcontent.com/pod-product-compliance
Lightning Source LLC
Chambersburg PA
CBHW070047100426
42740CB00013B/2830